The Unexpurgated Case Against Woman Suffrage

by Almroth E. Wright

CONTENTS

She May Attain Her Full Intellectual Stature.

ULTERIOR ENDS WHICH THE WOMAN'S SUFFRAGE MOVEMENT HAS IN VIEW

PART III

IS THERE, IF THE SUFFRAGE IS BARRED, ANY PALLIATIVE OR CORRECTIVE FOR THE DISCONTENTS OF WOMAN?

I

PALLIATIVES OR CORRECTIVES FOR THE DISCONTENT OF WOMAN

What are the Suffragist's Grievances?--Economic and Physiological Difficulties of Woman--Intellectual Grievances of Suffragist and Corrective.

APPENDIX

LETTER ON MILITANT HYSTERIA

PREFACE

It has come to be believed that everything that has a bearing upon the concession of the suffrage to woman has already been brought forward.

In reality, however, the influence of women has caused man to leave unsaid many things which he ought to have said.

Especially in two respects has woman restricted the discussion.

She has placed her taboo upon all generalisations about women, taking exception to these on the threefold ground that there would be no generalisations which would hold true of all women; that generalisations when reached possess no practical utility; and that the element of sex does not leave upon women any general imprint such as could properly be brought up in connexion with the question of admitting them to the electorate.

Woman has further stifled discussion by placing her taboo upon anything seriously unflattering being said about her in public.

I would suggest, and would propose here myself to act upon the suggestion, that, in connexion with the discussion of woman's suffrage, these restrictions should be laid aside.

In connexion with the setting aside of the restriction upon generalising, I may perhaps profitably point out that all generalisations, and not only generalisations which relate to women, are ex hypothesi [by hypothesis] subject to individual exceptions. (It is to generalisations that the proverb that "the exception proves the rule" really applies.) I may further point out that practically every decision which we take in ordinary life, and all legislative action without exception, is based upon generalisations; and again, that the question of the suffrage, and with it the larger question as to the proper sphere of woman, finally turns upon the question as to what imprint woman's sexual system leaves upon her physical frame, character, and intellect: in more technical terms, it turns upon the question as to what are the secondary sexual character[istic]s of woman.

Now only by a felicitous exercise of the faculty of successful generalisation can we arrive at a knowledge of these.

With respect to the restriction that nothing which might offend woman's amour propre [self love] shall be said in public, it may be pointed out that, while it was perfectly proper and equitable that no evil (and, as Pericles proposed, also no good) should be said of woman in public so long as she confined herself to the domestic sphere, the action of that section of women who have sought to effect an entrance into public life, has now brought down upon woman, as one of the penalties, the abrogation of that convention.

A consideration which perhaps ranks only next in importance to that with which we have been dealing, is that of the logical sanction of the propositions which are enunciated in the course of such controversial discussions as that in which we are here involved.

It is clearly a precondition of all useful discussion that the author and reader should be in accord with respect to the authority of the generalisations and definitions which supply the premisses for his reasonings.

Though this might perhaps to the reader appear an impractical ideal, I would propose here to attempt to reach it by explaining the logical method which I have set myself to follow.

Although I have from literary necessity employed in my text some of the verbal forms of dogmatism, I am very far from laying claim to any dogmatic authority. More than that, I would desire categorically to repudiate such a claim.

For I do not conceal from myself that, if I took up such a position, I should wantonly be placing myself at the mercy of my reader. For he could then, by merely refusing to see in me an authority, bring down the whole edifice of my argument like a house of cards.

Moreover I am not blind to what would happen if, after I claimed to be taken as an authority, the reader was indulgent enough still to go on to read what I have written.

He would in such a case, the moment he encountered a statement with which he disagreed, simply waive me on one side with the words, "So you say."

And if he should encounter a statement with which he agreed, he would in his wisdom, censure me for neglecting to provide for that proposition a satisfactory logical foundation.

If it is far from my thoughts to claim a right of dictation, it is equally remote from them to take up the position that I have in my arguments furnished proof of the thesis which I set out to establish.

It would be culpable misuse of language to speak in such connexion of proof or disproof.

Proof by testimony, which is available in con-nexion with questions of fact, is unavailable in connexion with general truths; and logical proof is obtainable only in that comparatively narrow sphere where reasoning is based--as in mathematics--upon axioms, or--as in certain really crucial experiments in the mathematic sciences--upon quasi- axiomatic premisses.

Everywhere else we base our reasonings on premises which are simply more or less probable; and accordingly the conclusions which we arrive at have in them always an element of insecurity.

It will be clear that in philosophy, in jurisprudence, in political economy and sociology, and in literary criticism and such like, we are dealing not with certainties but with propositions which are, for literary convenience, invested with the garb of certainties.

What kind of logical sanction is it, then, which can attach to reasonings such as are to be set out here?

They have in point of fact the sanction which attaches to reasonings based upon premises arrived at by the method of _diacritical judgment._

It is, I hasten to notify the reader, not the method, but only the name here assigned to it, which is unfamiliar. As soon as I exhibit it in the working, the reader will identify it as that by which every generalisation and definition ought to be put to the proof.

I may for this purpose take the general statements or definitions which serve as premisses for my reasonings in the text.

I bring forward those generalisations and definitions because they commend themselves to my diacritical judgment. In other words, I set them forth as results which have been reached after reiterated efforts to call up to mind the totality of my experience, and to de-tect the factor which is common to all the individual experiences.

When for instance I propose a definition, I have endeavoured to call to mind all the different uses of the word with which I am familiar--eliminating, of course, all the obviously incorrect uses.

And when I venture to attempt a generalisation about woman, I endeavour to recall to mind without distinction all the different women I have encountered, and to extricate from my impressions what was common to all,--omitting from consideration (except only when I am dealing specifically with these) all plainly abnormal women.

Having by this procedure arrived at a generalisation--which may of course be correct or incorrect--I submit it to my reader, and ask from him that he should, after going through the same mental operations as myself, review my judgment, and pronounce his verdict.

If it should then so happen that the reader comes, in the case of any generalisation, to the same verdict as that which I have reached, that particular generalisation will, I submit, now go forward not as a datum of my individual experience, but as the intellectual resultant of two separate and distinct experiences. It will thereby be immensely fortified.

If, on the other hand, the reader comes to the conclusion that a particular generalisation is out of conformity with his experience, that generalisation will go forward shorn of some, or perchance all, its authority.

But in any case each individual generalisation must be referred further.

And at the end it will, according as it finds, or fails to find, acceptance among the thoughtful, be endorsed as a truth, and be gathered into the garner of human knowledge; or be recognised as an error, and find its place with the tares, which the householder, in time of the harvest, will tell the reapers to bind in bundles to burn them.

A. E. W. 1913.

INTRODUCTION

Programme of this Treatise--Motives from which Women Claim the Suffrage--Types of Men who Support the Suffrage--John Stuart Mill.

The task which I undertake here is to show that the Woman's Suffrage Movement has no real intellectual or moral sanction, and that there are very weighty reasons why the suffrage should not be conceded to woman.

I would propose to begin by analysing the mental attitude of those who range themselves on the side of woman suffrage, and then to pass on to deal with the principal arguments upon which the woman suffragist relies.

The preponderating majority of the women who claim the suffrage do not do so from motives of public interest or philanthropy.

They are influenced almost exclusively by two motives: resentment at the suggestion that woman should be accounted by man as inherently his inferior in certain important respects; and reprehension of a state of society in which more money, more personal liberty (In reality only more of the personal liberty which the possession of money confers), more power, more public recognition and happier physiological conditions fall to the share of man.

A cause which derives its driving force so little from philanthropy and public interest and so much from offended amour propre and pretensions which are, as we shall see, unjustified, has in reality no moral prestige.

For its intellectual prestige the movement depends entirely on the fact that it has the advocacy of a certain number of distinguished men.

It will not be amiss to examine that advocacy.

The "intellectual" whose name appears at the foot of woman's suffrage petitions will, when you have him by himself, very often Make confession:-- "Woman suffrage," he will tell you, "is not the grave and important cause which the ardent female suffragist deems it to be. Not only will it not do any of the things which she imagines it is going to do, but it will leave the world exactly where it is. Still--the concession of votes to women is desirable from the point of view of symmetry of classification; and it will soothe the ruffled feelings of quite a number of very worthy women."

It may be laid down as a broad general rule that only two classes of men have the cause of woman's suffrage really at heart.

The first is the crank who, as soon as he thinks he has discerned a moral principle, immediately gets into the saddle, and then rides hell-for-leather, reckless of all considerations of public expediency.

The second is that very curious type of man, who when it is suggested in his hearing that the species woman is, measured by certain intellectual and moral standards, the inferior of the species man, solemnly draws himself up and asks, "Are you, sir, aware that you are insulting my wife?"

To this, the type of man who feels every unfavourable criticism of woman as a personal affront to himself, John Stuart Mill, had affinities.

We find him writing a letter to the Home Secretary, informing him, in relation to a Parliamentary Bill restricting the sale of arsenic to male persons over twenty-one years, that it was a "gross insult to every woman, all women from highest to lowest being deemed unfit to have poison in their possession, lest they shall commit murder."

We find him again, in a state of indignation with the English marriage laws, preluding his nuptials with Mrs. Taylor by presenting that lady with a formal charter; renouncing all authority over her, and promising her security against all infringements of her liberty which might proceed from himself.

To this lady he is always ascribing credit for his eminent intellectual achievements. And lest his reader should opine that woman stands somewhat in the shade with respect to her own intellectual triumphs, Mill undertakes the explanation. "Felicitous thoughts," he tells us, "occur by hundreds to every woman of intellect. But they are mostly lost for want of a husband or friend . . . to estimate them properly, and to bring them before the world; and even when they are brought before it they generally appear as his ideas."

Not only did Mill see woman and all her works through an optical medium which gave images like this; but there was upon his retina a large blind area. By reason of this last it was inapprehensible to him that there could be an objection to the sexes co-operating indiscriminately in work. It was beyond his ken that the sex element would under these conditions invade whole departments of life which are now free from it. As he saw things, there was in point of fact a risk of the human race dying out by reason of the inadequate imperativeness of its sexual instincts.

Mill's unfaithfulness to the facts cannot, however, all be put down to constitutional defects of vision. When he deals with woman he is no longer scrupulously conscientious. We begin to have our suspicions of his uprightness when we find him in his Subjection of Women laying it down as a fundamental postulate that the subjection of woman to man is always morally indefensible. For no upright mind can fail to see that the woman who lives in a condition of financial dependence upon man has no moral claim to unrestricted liberty. The suspicion of Mill's honesty which is thus awakened is confirmed by further critical reading of his treatise. In that skilful tractate one comes across, every here and there, a suggestio falsi [suggestion of a falsehood], or a suppressio veri [suppression of the truth], or a fallacious analogy nebulously expressed, or a mendacious metaphor, or a passage which is contrived to lead off attention from some weak point in the feminist case.[1] Moreover, Mill was unmindful of the obligations of intellectual morality when he allowed his stepdaughter, in connexion with feminist questions, to draft letters [2] which went forward as his own.

[1] Vide [See] in this connexion the incidental references to Mill on pp. 50, 81 footnote, and 139. [2] Vide Letters of John Stuart Mill, vol. ii, pp. 51, 79, 80, 100, 141, 157, 238, 239, 247, 288, and 349. There is yet another factor which must be kept in mind in connexion with the writings of Mill. It was the special

characteristic of the man to set out to tackle concrete problems and then to spend his strength upon abstractions.

In his Political Economy, where his proper subject matter was man with his full equipment of impulses, Mill took as his theme an abstraction: an economic man who is actuated solely by the desire of gain. He then worked out in great elaboration the course of conduct which an aggregate of these puppets of his imagination would pursue. Having persuaded

himself, after this, that he had in his possession a vade mecum [handbook] to the comprehension of human societies, he now took it upon himself to expound the principles which govern and direct these. Until such time as this procedure was unmasked, Mill's political economy enjoyed an unquestioned authority.

Exactly the same plan was followed by Mill in handling the question of woman's suffrage. Instead of dealing with woman as she is, and with woman placed in a setting of actually subsisting conditions, Mill takes as his theme a woman who is a creature of his imagination. This woman is, by assumption, in mental endowments a replica of man. She lives in a world which is, by tacit assumption, free from complications of sex. And, if practical considerations had ever come into the purview of Mill's mind, she would, by tacit assumption, be paying her own way, and be making full personal and financial contributions to the State. It is in connexion with this fictitious woman that Mill sets himself to work out the benefits which women would derive from co-partnership with men in the government of the State, and those which such co-partnership would confer on the community. Finally, practising again upon himself the same imposition as in his Political Economy, this unpractical trafficker in abstractions sets out to persuade his reader that he has, by dealing with fictions of the mind, effectively grappled with the concrete problem of woman's suffrage.

This, then, is the philosopher who gives intellectual prestige to the Woman's Suffrage cause.

But is there not, let us in the end ask ourselves, here and there at least, a man who is of real account in the world of affairs, and who is--not simply a luke-warm Platonic friend or an opportunist advocate--but an impassioned promoter of the woman's suffrage movement? One knows quite well that there is. But then one suspects --one perhaps discerns by "the spirit sense"-- that this impassioned promoter of woman's suffrage is, on the sequestered side of his life, an idealistic dreamer: one for whom some woman's memory has become, like Beatrice for Dante, a mystic religion.

We may now pass on to deal with the arguments by which the woman suffragist has sought to establish her case.

PART I

ARGUMENTS WHICH ARE ADDUCED IN SUPPORT OF WOMAN'S SUFFRAGE

I

ARGUMENTS FROM ELEMENTARY NATURAL RIGHTS

Signification of the Term "Woman's Rights"--Argument from "Justice" -- Juridical Justice-"Egalitarian Equity"--Argument from Justice Applied to Taxation--Argument from Liberty--Summary of Arguments from Elementary Natural Rights.

Let us note that the suffragist does not--except, perhaps, when she is addressing herself to unfledged girls and to the sexually embittered--really produce much effect by inveighing against the legal grievances of woman under the bastardy laws, the divorce laws, and the law which fixes the legal age of consent. This kind of appeal does not go down with the ordinary man and woman--first, because there are many who think that in spite of occasional hardships the public advantage is, on the whole, very well served by the existing laws; secondly, because any alterations which might be desirable could very easily be made without recourse to woman's suffrage; and thirdly, because the suffragist consistently acts on the principle of bringing up against man everything that can possibly be brought up against him, and of never allowing anything to appear on the credit side of the ledger.

The arguments which the woman suffragist really places confidence in are those which are provided by undefined general principles, apothegms set out in the form of axioms, formulae which are vehicles for fallacies, ambiguous abstract terms, and "question-begging" epithets. Your ordinary unsophisticated man and woman stand almost helpless against arguments of this kind.

For these bring to bear moral pressure upon human nature. And when the intellect is confused by a word or formula which conveys an ethical appeal, one may very easily find oneself committed to action which one's unbiased reason would never have approved. The very first requirement in connexion with any word or phrase which conveys a moral exhortation is, therefore, to analyse it and find out its true signification. For all such concepts as justice, rights, freedom, chivalry--and it is with these that we shall be specially concerned--are, when properly defined and understood beacon-lights, but when ill understood and undefined, stumbling-blocks in the path of humanity.

We may appropriately begin by analysing the term "Woman's Rights" and the correlative formula "Woman has a right to the suffrage."

Our attention here immediately focuses upon the term right. It is one of the most important of the verbal agents by which the suffragist hopes to bring moral pressure to bear upon man.

Now, the term right denotes in its juridical sense a debt which is owed to us by the State. A right is created when the community binds itself to us, its individual members, to intervene by force to restrain any one from interfering with us, and to protect us in the enjoyment of our faculties, privileges, and property.

The term is capable of being given a wider meaning. While no one could appropriately speak of our having a right to health or anything that man has not the power to bestow, it is arguable that there are, independent of and antecedent to law, elementary rights: a right to freedom; a right to protection against personal violence; a right to the protection of our property; and a right to the impartial administration of regulations which are binding upon all. Such a use of the term right could be justified on the ground that everybody would be willing to make personal sacrifices, and to combine with his fellows for the purpose of securing these essentials--an understanding which would almost amount to legal sanction.

The suffragist who employs the term "Woman's Rights" does not employ the word rights in either of these senses. Her case is analogous to that of a man who should in a republic argue about the divine right of kings; or that of the Liberal who should argue that it was his right to live permanently under a Liberal government; or of any member of a minority who should, with a view of getting what he wants, argue that he was contending only for his rights.

The woman suffragist is merely bluffing. Her formula "_Woman's Rights" means simply "Woman's Claims_."

For the moment--for we shall presently be coming back to the question of the enforcement of rights--our task is to examine the arguments which the suffragist brings forward in support of her claims.

First and chief among these is the argument that the _Principle of Justice_ prescribes that women should be enfranchised.

When we inquire what the suffragist understands under the Principle of Justice, one receives by way of answer only the _petitio principii [question begging]_ that Justice is a moral principle which includes woman suffrage among its implications.

In reality it is only very few who clearly apprehend the nature of Justice. For under this appellation two quite different principles are confounded.

The primary and correct signification of the term Justice will perhaps be best arrived at by pursuing the following train of considerations:--

When man, long impatient at arbitrary and quite incalculable autocratic judgments, proceeded to build up a legal system to take the place of these, he built it upon the following series of axioms:--(a) All actions of which the courts are to take cognisance shall be classified. (b) The legal consequences of each class of action shall be definitely fixed. (c) The courts shall adjudicate only on questions of fact, and on the issue as to how the particular deed which is the cause of action should be classified. And (d) such decisions shall carry with them in an automatic manner the appointed legal consequences.

For example, if a man be arraigned for the appropriation of another man's goods, it is an axiom that the court (when once the questions of fact have been disposed of) shall adjudicate only on the issue as to whether the particular appropriation of goods in dispute comes under the denomination of larceny, burglary, or other co-ordinate category; and that upon this the sentence shall go forth: directing that the legal consequences which are appointed to that particular class of action be enforced.

This is the system every one can see administered in every court of justice.

There is, however, over and above what has just been set out another essential element in Justice. It is an element which readily escapes the eye.

I have in view the fact that the classifications which are adopted and embodied in the law must not be arbitrary classifications. They must all be conformable to the principle of utility, and be directed to the advantage of society.

If, for instance, burglary is placed in a class apart from larceny, it is discriminated from it because this distinction is demanded by considerations of public advantage. But considerations of utility would not countenance, and by consequence Justice would not accept, a classification of theft into theft committed by a poor man and theft committed by a rich man.

The conception of Justice is thus everywhere interfused with considerations of utility and expediency.

It will have become plain that if we have in view the justice which is administered in the courts--we may here term it _Juridical Justice--then the question as to whether it is just_ to refuse the suffrage to woman will be determined by considering whether the classification of men as voters and of women as non-voters is in the public interest. Put otherwise, the question whether it would be just that woman should have a vote would require the answer "Yes" or "No," according as the question whether it would be expedient or inexpedient that woman should vote required the answer "Yes" or "No." But it would be for the electorate, not for the woman suffragist, to decide that question.

There is, as already indicated, another principle which passes under the name of Justice. I have in view the principle that in the distribution of wealth or political power, or any other privileges which it is in the power of the State to bestow, every man should share equally with every other man, and every woman equally with every man, and that in countries where Europeans and natives live side by side, these latter should share all privileges equally with the white--the goal of endeavour being that all distinctions depending upon natural endowment, sex, and race should be effaced.

We may call this principle the _Principle of Egalitarian Equity_--first, because it aims at establishing a quite artificial equality; secondly, because it makes appeal to our ethical instincts, and claims on that ground to override the distinctions of which formal law takes account.

But let us reflect that we have here a principle which properly understood, embraces in its purview all mankind, and not mankind only but also the lower animals. That is to say, we have here a principle, which consistently followed out, would make of every man and woman _in primis [at first]_ a socialist; then a woman suffragist; then a philo-native, negrophil, and an advocate of the political rights of natives and negroes; and then, by logical compulsion ant anti-vivisectionist, who accounts it unjust to experiment on an animal; a vegetarian, who accounts it unjust to kill animals for food; and findly one who, like the Jains, accounts it unjust to take the life of even verminous insects.

If we accept this principle of egalitarian equity as of absolute obligation, we shall have to accept along with woman's suffrage all the other "isms" believed in, and agitated for, by the cranks who are so numerously represented in the ranks of woman suffragists.

If, on the other hand, we accept the doctrine of egalitarian equity with the qualification that it shall apply only so far as what it enjoins is conformable to public advantage, we shall again make expediency the criterion of the justice of woman's suffrage.

Before passing on it will be well to point out that the argument from Justice meets us not only in the form that Justice requires that woman should have a vote, but also in all sorts of other forms. We encounter it in the writings of publicists, in the formula Taxation _carries with it a Right to Representation_; and we encounter it in the streets, on the banners of woman suffrage processions, in the form Taxation without Representation is Tyranny.

This latter theorem of taxation which is displayed on the banners of woman suffrage is, I suppose, deliberately and intentionally a suggestio falsi. For only that taxation is tyrannous which is diverted to objects which are not useful to the contributors. And even the suffragist does not suggest that the taxes which are levied on women are differentially applied to the uses of men.

Putting, then, this form of argument out of sight, let us come to close quarters with the question whether the payment of taxes gives a title to control the finances of the State.

Now, if it really did so without any regard to the status of the claimant, not only women, but also foreigners residing in, or holding property in, England, and with these lunatics and miners with property, and let me, for the sake of a pleasanter collocation of ideas, hastily add peers of the realm, who have now no control over public finance, ought to receive the parliamentary franchise. And in like manner if the payment of a tax, without consideration of its amount, were to give a title to a vote, every one who bought an article which had paid a duty would be entitled to a vote in his own, or in a foreign, country according as that duty has been paid at home or abroad.

In reality the moral and logical nexus between the payment of taxes and the control of the public revenue is that the solvent and selfsupporting citizens, and only these, are entitled to direct its financial policy.

If I have not received, or if I have refunded, any direct contributions I may have received from the coffers of the State; if I have paid my pro rata share of its establishment charges--i.e. of the costs of both internal administration and external defence; and I have further paid my proportional share of whatever may be required to make up for the deficit incurred on account of my fellow-men and women who either require direct assistance from the State, or cannot meet their share of the expenses of the State, I am a solvent citizen; and if I fail to meet these liabilities, I am an insolvent citizen even though I pay such taxes as the State insists upon my paying.

Now if a woman insists, in the face of warnings that she had better not do so, on taxing man with dishonesty for withholding from her financial control over the revenues of the State, she has only herself to blame if she is told very bluntly that her claim to such control is barred by the fact that she is, as a citizen insolvent. The taxes paid by women would cover only a, very small proportion of the establishment charges of the State which would properly be assigned to them. It falls to man to make up that deficit.

And it is to be noted with respect to those women who pay their full pro rata contribution and who ask to be treated as a class apart from, and superior to, other women, that only a very small proportion of these have made their position for themselves.

Immeasurably the larger number are in a solvent position only because men have placed them there. All large fortunes and practically all the incomes which are furnished by investments are derived from man.

Nay; but the very revenues which the Woman Suffrage Societies devote to man's vilification are to a preponderating extent derived from funds which he earned and gave over to woman.

In connexion with the financial position of woman as here stated, it will be well to consider first the rich woman's claim to the vote.

We may seek light on the logical and moral aspects of this claim by considering here two parallel cases.

The position which is occupied by the peer under the English Constitution furnishes a very interesting parallel to the position of the woman who is here in question.

Time out of mind the Commons have viewed with the utmost jealousy any effort of the House of Lords to obtain co-partnership with them in the control of the finances of the State; and, in pursuance of that traditional policy, the peers have recently, after appeal to the country, been shorn of the last vestige of financial control. Now we may perhaps see, in this jealousy of a House of Lords, which represents inherited wealth, displayed by a House of Commons representing voters electing on a financial qualification, an unconscious groping after the moral principle that those citizens who are solvent by their own efforts, and only these, should control the finances of the State.

And if this analogy finds acceptance, it would not--even if there were nothing else than this against such proposals--be logically possible, after ousting the peers who are large tax-payers from all control over the finances of the State, to create a new class of voters out of the female representatives of unearned wealth.

The second parallel case which we have to consider presents a much simpler analogy. Consideration will show that the position occupied in the State by the woman who has inherited money is analogous to that occupied in a firm by a sleeping partner who stands in the shoes of a deceased working partner, and who has only a small amount of capital in the business. Now, if such a partner were to claim any financial control, and were to make trouble about paying his pro rata establishment charges, he would be very sharply called to order. And he would never dream of appealing to Justice by breaking windows, going to gaol, and undertaking a hunger strike.

Coming back from the particular to the general, and from the logical to the moral aspect of woman's claim to control the finances of the State on the ground that she is a tax-payer, it will suffice to point out that this claim is on a par with the claim to increased political power and completer control over the finances of the State which is put forward by a class of male voters who are already paying much less than their pro rata share of the upkeep of the State.

In each case it is a question of trying to get control of other people's money. And in the case of woman it is of "trying on" in connexion with her public partnership with man that principle of domestic partnership, "All yours is mine, and all mine's my own."

Next to the plea of justice, the plea which is advanced most insistently by the woman who is contending for a vote is the plea of liberty.

We have here, again, a word which is a valuable asset to woman suffrage both in the respect that it brings moral pressure to bear, and in the respect that it is a word of ambiguous meaning.

In accordance with this we have John Stuart Mill making propaganda for woman suffrage in a tractate entitled the Subjection of Women; we have a Woman's Freedom League--"freedom" being a question-begging synonym for "parliamentary franchise"--and everywhere in the literature of woman's suffrage we have talk of woman's "emancipation"; and we have women characterised as serfs, or slaves--the terms serfs and slaves supplying, of course, effective rhetorical synonyms for non-voters.

When we have succeeded in getting through these thick husks of untruth we find that the idea of liberty which floats before the eyes of woman is, not at all a question of freedom from unequitable legal restraints, but essentially a question of getting more of the personal liberty (or command of other people's services), which the possession of money confers and more freedom from sexual restraints.

The suffragist agitator makes profit out of this ambiguity. In addressing the woman worker who does not, at the rate which her labour commands on the market, earn enough to give her any reasonable measure of financial freedom, the agitator will assure her that the suffrage would bring her more money, describing the woman suffrage cause to her as the cause of liberty. By juggling in this way with the two meanings of "liberty" she will draw her into her toils.

The vote, however, would not raise wages of the woman worker and bring to her the financial, nor yet the physiological freedom she is seeking.

The tactics of the suffragist agitator are the same when she is dealing with a woman who is living at the charges of a husband or relative, and who recoils against the idea that she lies under a moral obligation to make to the man who works for her support some return of gratitude. The suffragist agitator will point out to her that such an obligation is slavery, and that the woman's suffrage cause is the cause of freedom.

And so we find the women who want to have everything for nothing, and the wives who do not see that they are beholden to man for anything, and those who consider that they have not made a sufficiently good bargain for themselves--in short, all the ungrateful women--flock to the banner of Women's Freedom--the banner of financial freedom for woman at the expense of financial servitude for man.

The grateful woman will practically always be an anti-suffragist.

It will be well, before passing on to another class of arguments, to summarise what has been said in the three foregoing sections.

We have recognised that woman has not been defrauded of elementary natural rights; that Justice, as distinguished from egalitarian equity, does not prescribe that she should be admitted to the suffrage; and that her status is not, as is dishonestly alleged, a status of serfdom or slavery.

With this the whole case for recrimination against man, and _a fortiori [for greater reason]_ the case for [a] resort to violence, collapses.

And if it does collapse, this is one of those things that carries consequences. It would beseem man to bethink himself that to give in to an unjustified and doubtfully honest claim is to minister to the demoralisation of the claimant.

II

ARGUMENTS FROM INTELLECTUAL GRIEVANCES OF WOMAN

Complaint of Want of Chivalry--Complaint of "Insults"--Complaint of "Illogicalities"--Complaint of "Prejudices"--The Familiar Suffragist Grievance of the Drunkard Voter and the Woman of Property Who is a Non-Voter--The Grievance of Woman being Required to Obey Man-Made Laws.

We pass from the argument from elementary natural rights to a different class of arguments--intellectual grievances. The suffragist tells us that it is unchivalrous to oppose woman's suffrage; that it is insulting to tell woman that she is unfit to exercise the fran- chise; that it is "illogical" to make in her case an exception to a general rule; that it is mere "prejudice" to withhold the vote from her; that it is indignity that the virtuous and highly intelligent woman has no vote, while the drunkard has; and that the woman of property has no vote, while her male underlings have; and, lastly, that it is an affront that a woman should be required to obey "man-made" laws.

We may take these in their order.

Let us consider chivalry, first, from the standpoint of the woman suffragist. Her notion of chivalry is that man should accept every disadvantageous offer which may be made to him by woman.

That, of course, is to make chivalry the principle of egalitarian equity limited in its application to the case between man and woman.

It follows that she who holds that the suffrage ought, in obedience to that principle of justice, to be granted to her by man, might quite logically hold that everything else in man's gift ought also to be conceded.

But to do the woman suffragist justice, she does not press the argument from chivalry. Inasmuch as life has brought home to her that the ordinary man has quite other conceptions of that virtue, she declares that "she has no use for it."

Let us now turn to the anti-suffragist view. The anti-suffragist (man or woman) holds that chivalry is a principle which enters into every reputable relation between the sexes, and that of all the civilising agencies at work in the world it is the most important.

But I think I hear the reader interpose, "What, then, is chivalry if it is not a question of serving woman without reward?"

A moment's thought will make the matter clear.

When a man makes this compact with a woman, "I will do you reverence, and protect you, and yield you service; and you, for your part, will hold fast to an ideal of gentleness, of personal refinement, of modesty, of joyous maternity, and to who shall say what other graces and virtues that endear woman to man," that is chivalry.

It is not a question of a purely one-sided bargain, as in the suffragist conception. Nor yet is it a bargain about purely material things.

It is a bargain in which man gives both material things, and also things which pertain perhaps somewhat to the spirit; and in which woman gives back of these last.

But none the less it is of the nature of a contract. There is in it the inexorable _do ut des; facio ut facias [give me this, and I will give you that; do this for me, and I will do that for you]._

And the contract is infringed when woman breaks out into violence, when she jettisons her personal refinement, when she is ungrateful, and, possibly, when she places a quite extravagantly high estimate upon her intellectual powers.

We now turn from these almost too intimate questions of personal morality to discuss the other grievances which were enumerated above.

With regard to the suffragist's complaint that it is "insulting" for woman to be told that she is as a class unfit to exercise the suffrage, it is relevant to point out that one is not insulted by being told about oneself, or one's class, untruths, but only at being told about oneself, or one's class, truths which one dislikes. And it is, of course, an offence against ethics to try to dispose of an unpalatable generalisation by characterising it as "insulting." But nothing that man could do would be likely to prevent the suffragist resorting to this aggravated form of intellectual immorality.

We may now turn to the complaint that it is "illogical" to withhold the vote from women.

This is the kind of complaint which brings out in relief the logical endowment and legislative sagacity of the suffragist.

With regard to her logical endowment it will suffice to indicate that the suffragist would appear to regard the promulgation of a rule which is to hold without exception as an essentially logical act; and the admission of any class exception to a rule of general application as an illogicality. It would on this principle be "illogical" to except, under conscription, the female population from military service.

With regard to the suffragist's legislative sagacity we may note that she asks that we should put back the clock, and return to the days when any arbitrary principle might be adduced as a ground for legislation. It is as if Bentham had never taught:--

"What is it to offer a good reason with respect to a law? It is to allege the good or evil which the law tends to produce; so much good, so many arguments in its favour; so much evil, so many arguments against it.

"What is it to offer a false reason? It is the alleging for, or against a law, something else than its good or evil effects."

Next, we may take up the question as to whether an unwelcome generalisation may legitimately be got out of the way by characterising it as a prejudice. This is a fundamentally important question not only in connexion with such an issue as woman suffrage, but in connexion with all search for truth in those regions where crucial scientific experiments cannot be instituted.

In the whole of this region of thought we have to guide ourselves by generalisations.

Now every generalisation is in a sense a prejudgment. We make inferences from cases or individuals that have already presented themselves to such cases or individuals of the same class as may afterwards present themselves. And if our generalisation happens to be an unfavourable one, we shall of necessity have prejudged the case against those who are exceptions to their class.

Thus, for example, the proposition that woman is incapable of usefully exercising the parliamentary franchise prejudges the case against a certain number of capable women. It would none the less be absolutely anarchical to propose to abandon the system of guiding ourselves by prejudgments; and unfavourable prejudgments or prejudices are logically as well justified, and are obviously as indispensable to us as favourable prejudgments.

The suffragist who proposes to dispose of generalisations which are unfavourable to woman as prejudices ought therefore to be told to stand down.

It has probably never suggested itself to her that, if there were a mind which was not stored with both favourable prejudgments and prejudices, it would be a mind which had learned absolutely nothing from experience.

But I hear the reader interpose, "Is there not a grave danger that generalisations may be erroneous?"

And I can hear the woman suffragist interject, "Is there not a grave danger that unflattering generalisations about woman may be erroneous?"

The answer to the general question is that there is of course always the risk that our generalisations may be erroneous. But when a generalisation finds wide acceptance among the thoughtful, we have come as close to truth as it is possible for humanity to come.

To the question put by the suffragist the reply is that experience with regard to the capacity of woman has been accumulating in all climes, and through all times; and that the belief of men in the inherent inferiority of women in the matter of intellectual morality, and in the power of adjudication, has never varied.

I pass now to the two most familiar grievances of the suffragist; the grievance that the virtuous and intelligent woman has no vote, while the male drunkard has; and the grievance that the woman of property has no vote, while her male underlings have.

All that is worth while saying on these points is that the suffragist is here manufacturing grievances for herself, first, by reasoning from the false premiss that every legal distinction which happens to press hardly upon a few individuals ought for that to be abrogated; and, secondly, by steady leaving out of sight that logical inconsistencies can, for the more part, be got rid of only at the price of bringing others into being.

The man who looks forward to the intellectual development of woman must be brought near to despair when he perceives that practically every woman suffragist sees in every hard case arising in connexion with a legal distinction affecting woman, an insult and example of the iniquity of man-made laws, or a logical inconsistency which could with a very little good-will be removed.

We have come now to the last item on our list, to the grievance that woman has to submit herself to "man-made laws."

This is a grievance which well rewards study. It is worth study from the suffragist point of view, because it is the one great injury under which all others are subsumed. And it is worth studying from the anti-suffragist point of view, because it shows how little the suffragist understands of the terms she employs; and how unreal are the wrongs which she resents.

Quite marvelously has the woman suffragist in this connexion misapprehended; or would she have us say misrepresented?

The woman suffragist misapprehends--it will be better to assume that she "misapprehends"--when she suggests that we, the male electors, have framed the laws.

In reality the law which we live under--and the law in those States which have adopted either the English, or the Roman law--descends from the past. It has been evolved precedent, by precedent, by the decisions of generation upon generation of judges, and it has for centuries been purged by amending statutes. Moreover we, the present male electors--the electors who are savagely attacked by the suffragist for our asserted iniquities in connexion with the laws which regulate sexual relations--have never in our capacity as electors had any power to alter an old, or to suggest a new law; except only in so far as by voting Conservative or Liberal we may indirectly have remotely influenced the general trend of legislation.

"Well but"--the suffragist will here rejoin--"is it not at any rate true that in the drafting of statutes and the framing of judicial decisions man has always nefariously discriminated against woman?"

The question really supplies its own answer. It will be obvious to every one who considers that the drafting of statutes and the formulating of legal decisions is almost as impersonal a procedure as that of drawing up the rules to govern a game; and it offers hardly more opportunity for discriminating between man and woman.

There are, however, three questions in connexion with which the law can and does make a distinction between man and woman.

The first is that of sexual relations: rape, divorce, bastardy, and the age of consent. In connexion with rape, it has never been alleged that the law is not sufficiently severe. It is, or has been, under colonial conditions, severe up to the point of ferocity. In the matter of divorce the law of a minority of man-governed States differentiates in favour of man. It does so influenced by tradition, by what are held to be the natural equities, and by the fact that a man is required to support his wife's progeny. The law of _bastardy [illegitimate childbirth]_ is what it is because of the dangers of blackmail. The law which fixes the age of consent discriminates against man, laying him open to a criminal charge in situations where woman--and it is not certain that she is not a more frequent offender--escapes scot-free.

The second point in which the law differentiates is in the matter of exacting personal service for the State. If it had not been that man is more prone to discriminate in favour of woman than against her, every military State, when exacting personal military service from men, would have demanded from women some such equivalent personal service as would be represented by a similar period of work in an army clothing establishment, or ordnance factory, or army laundry; or would at any rate have levied upon woman a ransom in lieu of such service.

The third point in which the law distinguishes between man and woman is with reference to the suffrage. The object of this book is to show that this is equitable and in the interests of both.

The suffragist further misapprehends when she regards it as an indignity to obey laws which she has not herself framed, or specifically sanctioned. (The whole male electorate, be it remarked, would here lie under the same dignity as woman.)

But in reality, whether it is a question of the rules of a game, or of the reciprocal rights and duties of members of a community, it is, and ought to be, to every reasonable human being not a grievance, but a matter of felicitation, that an expert or a body of experts should have evolved a set of rules under which order and harmony are achieved. Only vanity and folly would counsel amateurs to try to draw up rules or laws for themselves.

Again, the woman suffragist takes it as a matter of course that she would herself be able to construct a system of workable laws. In point of fact, the framing of a really useful law is a question of divining something which will apply to an infinite number of different cases and individuals. It is an intellectual feat on a par with the framing of a great generalisation. And would woman--that being of such short sight, whose mind is always so taken up with whatever instances lie nearest to her--be capable of framing anything that could pass muster as a great generalisation?

Lastly, the suffragist fails to see that the function of framing the laws is not an essential function of citizenship.

The essential functions of citizenship are the shaping of public policy, and the control of the administrative Acts of Government.

Such directive control is in a state of political freedom exercised through two quite different agencies.

It is exercised--and it is of the very essence of political freedom that this should be the normal method of control--in the first place, through expressed public opinion. By this are continuously regulated not only momentous matters of State, such as declarations of war and the introduction of constitutional changes, but also smaller and more individual matters, such as the commutation of a capital sentence, or the forcible feeding of militant suffragists.

In the background, behind the moral compulsion of expressed public opinion, there is, in the case of a Parliamentary State, also another instrument of control. I have in view that periodical settlement of the contested rulership of the State by the force of a majority of electors which is denoted a general election.

The control exercised by the suffrages of the electors in a general election is in certain important respects less effective than that exercised by the everyday public expression of opinion. It falls short in the respect that its verdicts are, except only in connexion with the issue as to whether the Government is to be retained in office or dismissed, ambiguous verdicts; further, in the respect that it comes into application either before governmental proposals have taken definite shape, or only after the expiration of a term of years, when the events are already passing out of memory.

If we now consider the question of woman's franchise from the wider point of view here opened up, it will be clear that, so far as concerns the control which is exercised through public opinion on the Government, the intelligent woman, and especially the intelligent woman who has made herself an expert on any matter, is already in possession of that which is a greater power than the franchise. She has the power which attaches to all intelligent opinion promulgated in a free State. Moreover, wherever the special interest of women are involved, any woman may count on being listened to if she is voicing the opinions of any considerable section of her sex.

In reality, therefore, woman is disfranchised only so far as relates to the confirmation of a Government in office, or its dismissal by the ultima ratio [ultimate reason] of an electoral contest. And when we reflect that woman does not come into consideration as a compelling force, and that an electoral contest partakes of the nature of a civil war, it becomes clear that to give her the parliamentary vote would be to reduce all those trials of strength which take the form of electoral contests to the level of a farce.

With this I have, I will not say completed the tale of the suffragist's grievances--that would be impossible--but I have at any rate dealt with those which she has most acrimoniously insisted upon.

III

ARGUMENTS WHICH TAKE THE FORM OF "COUNSELS OF PERFECTION" ADDRESSED TO MAN

Argument that Woman Requires a Vote for her Protection--Argument that Woman ought to be Invested with the Responsibilities of Voting in Order that She May Attain Her Full Intellectual Stature.

There, however, remains still a further class of arguments. I have in view here arguments which have nothing to do with elementary natural rights, nor yet with wounded amour propre. They concern ethics, and sympathy, and charitable feelings.

The suffragist here gives to man "counsels of perfection."

It will be enough to consider here two of these:--the first, the argument that woman, being the weaker vessel, needs, more than man, the suffrage for her protection; the second, that woman, being less than man in relation to public life, ought to be given the vote for instructional purposes.

The first of these appeals will, for instance, take the following form:-- "Consider the poor sweated East End woman worker. She knows best where the shoe pinches. You men can't know. Give her a vote; and you shall see that she will very soon better her condition."

When I hear that argument I consider:--We will suppose that woman was ill. Should we go to her and say: "You know best, know better than any man, what is wrong with you. Here are all the medicines and remedies. Make your own selection, for that will assuredly provide what will be the most likely to help."

If this would be both futile and inhuman, much more would it be so to seek out this woman who is sick in fortune and say to her, "Go and vote for the parliamentary candidate who will be likely to influence the trend of legislation in a direction which will help."

What would really help the sweated woman labourer would, of course, be to have the best intellect brought to bear, not specially upon the problem of indigent woman, but upon the whole social problem.

But the aspect of the question which is, from our present point of view, the fundamentally important one is the following: Granting that the extension of the suffrage to woman would enable her, as the suffragist contends, to bring pressure upon her parliamentary representative, man, while anxious to do his very best for woman, might very reasonably refuse to go about it in this particular way.

If a man has a wife whom he desires to treat indulgently, he does not necessarily open a joint account with her at his bankers.

If he wants to contribute to a charity he does not give to the managers of that charity a power of attorney over his property.

And if he is a philanthropical director of a great business he does not, when a pathetic case of poverty among his staff is brought to his notice, imperil the fortunes of his undertaking by giving to his workmen shares and a vote in the management.

Moreover, he would perhaps regard it as a little suspect if a group of those who were claiming this as a right came and told him that "it was very selfish of him" not to grant their request.

Precious above rubies to the suffragist and every other woman who wants to apply the screw to man is that word selfish. It furnishes her with the petitio principii that man is under an ethical obligation to give anything she chooses to ask.

We come next--and this is the last of all the arguments we have to consider--to the argument that the suffrage ought to be given to woman for instructional purposes.

Now it would be futile to attempt to deny that we have ready to hand in the politics of the British Empire--that Empire which is swept along in "the too vast orb of her fate"--an ideal political training-ground in which we might put woman to school. The woman voter would there be able to make any experiment she liked.

But one wonders why it has not been proposed to carry woman's instruction further, and for instructional purposes to make of a woman let us say a judge, or an ambassador, or a Prime Minister.

There would--if only it were legitimate to sacrifice vital national interests--be not a little to say in favour of such a course. One might at any rate hope by these means once for all to bring home to man the limitations of woman.

PART II

ARGUMENTS AGAINST THE CONCESSION OF THE PARLIAMENTARY SUFFRAGE TO

WOMAN

I

WOMAN'S DISABILITY IN THE MATTER OF PHYSICAL FORCE

International Position of State would be Imperilled by Woman's Suffrage--Internal Equilibrium of State would be Imperilled.

The woman suffrage movement has now gone too far to be disposed of by the overthrow of its arguments, and by a mere indication of those which could be advanced on the other side. The situation demands the bringing forward of the case against woman's suffrage; and it must be the full and quite unexpurgated case.

I shall endeavour to do this in the fewest possible words, and to be more especially brief where I have to pass again over ground which I have previously traversed in dealing with the arguments of the suffragists.

I may begin with what is fundamental. It is an axiom that we should in legislating guide ourselves directly by considerations of utility and expediency. For abstract principles--I have in view here _rights, justice, egalitarian equity, equality, liberty, chivalry, logicality,_ and such like--are not all of them guides to utility; and each of these is, as we have seen, open to all manner of private misinterpretation.

Applying the above axiom to the issue before us, it is clear that we ought to confine ourselves here to the discussion of the question as to whether the State would, or would not, suffer from the admission of women to the electorate.

We can arrive at a judgment upon this by considering, on the one hand, the class-characters of women so far as these may be relevant to the question of the suffrage; and, on the other hand, the legislative programmes put forward by the female legislative reformer and the feminist.

In connexion with the class-characters of woman, it will be well, before attempting to indicate them, to interpolate here the general consideration that the practical statesman, who has to deal with things as they are, is not required to decide whether the characters of women which will here be considered are, as the physiologist (who knows that the sexual products influence every tissue of the body) cannot doubt, "secondary sexual characters"; or, as the suffragist contends, "acquired characters." It will be plain that whether defects are "secondary sexual characters" (and therefore as irremediable as "racial characters"); or whether they are "acquired characters" (and as such theoretically remediable) they are relevant to the question of the concession of the suffrage just so long as they continue to be exhibited.[1]

[1] This is a question on which Mill (vide Subjection of Women, last third of Chapter I) has endeavoured to confuse the issues for his reader, first, by representing that by no possibility can man know anything of the "nature," i.e., of the "secondary sexual characters" of woman; and, secondly, by distracting attention from the fact that "acquired characters" may produce unfitness for the suffrage.

The primordial argument against giving woman the vote is that that vote would not represent physical force.

Now it is by physical force alone and by prestige--which represents physical force in the background--that a nation protects itself against foreign interference, upholds its rule over subject populations, and enforces its own laws. And nothing could in the end more certainly lead to war and revolt than the decline of the military spirit and loss of prestige which would inevitably follow if man admitted woman into political co-partnership.

While it is arguable that such a partnership with woman in government as obtains in Australia and New Zealand is sufficiently unreal to be endurable, there cannot be two opinions on the question that a virile and imperial race will not brook any attempt at forcible control by women.

Again, no military foreign nation or native race would ever believe in the stamina and firmness of purpose of any nation that submitted even to the semblance of such control.

The internal equilibrium of the State also would be endangered by the admission to the register of millions of electors whose vote would not be endorsed by the authority of physical force.

Regarded from this point of view a Woman's Suffrage measure stands on an absolutely different basis to any other extension of the suffrage. An extension which takes in more men--whatever else it may do--makes for stability in the respect that it makes the decrees of the legislature more irresistible. An extension which takes in any women undermines the physical sanction of the laws.

We can see indications of the evil that would follow such an event in the profound dissatisfaction which is felt when--in violation of the democratic principle that every man shall count for one, and no man for more than one-- the political wishes of the large constituencies which return relatively few members to Parliament, are overborne by those of constituencies which, with a smaller aggregate population, return more members.

And we see what such evil finally culminates in when the over-representation of one part of a country and the corresponding under-representation of other portions has led a large section of the people to pledge themselves to disregard the eventual ordinances of Parliament.

If ever the question as to whether the will of Ulster or that of the Nationalists is to prevail is brought to the arbitrament of physical force, it will be due to the inequalities of parliamentary representation as between England and Ireland, and as between the Unionist and Nationalist population of Ulster.

The general lesson that all governmental action ought to be backed by force, is further brought home to the conscience when we take note of the fact that every one feels that public morality is affronted when senile, infirm, and bedridden men are brought to the poll to turn the scale in hotly contested elections.

For electoral decisions are felt to have moral prestige only when the electoral figures quantitatively represent the physical forces which are engaged on either side. And where vital interests are involved, no class of men can be expected to accept any decision other than one which rests upon the ultima ratio.

Now all the evils which are the outcome of disparities between the parliamentary power and the organised physical force of contending parties would "grow" a hundredfold if women were admitted to the suffrage.

There would after that be no electoral or parliamentary decision which would not be open to challenge on the ground that it was impossible to tell whether the party which came out the winner had a majority which could enforce its will, or only a majority obtained by the inclusion of women. And no measure of redistribution could ever set that right.

There may find place here also the consideration that the voting of women would be an unsettling element in the government of the State, forasmuch as they would, by reason of a general lack of interest in public affairs, only very; seldom come to the poll: would, in fact, come to the poll in full strength only when some special appeal had come home to their emotions.

Now an electorate which includes a very large proportion of quite uninterested voters would be in the same case as a legislature which included a very large proportion of members who made a practice of staying away. It would be in the same case, because the absentees, who would not have acquired the training which comes from consecutive attention to public affairs, might at any moment step in and upset the stability of State by voting for some quite unconsidered measure.

Coming back in conclusion to our main issue, I would re-emphasise an aspect of the question upon which I have already elsewhere insisted.[1] I have in view the fact that woman does, and should, stand to physical violence in a fundamentally different relation to man. Nothing can alter the fact that, the very moment woman resorts to violence, she places herself within the jurisdiction of an ethical law, which is as old as civilisation, and which was framed in its interests.

[1] Vide Appendix, pp. 176-179.

II

WOMAN'S DISABILITY IN THE MATTER OF INTELLECT

Characteristics of the Feminine Mind--Suffragist Illusions with Regard to the Equality of Man and Woman as Workers--Prospect for the Intellectual Future of Woman--Has Woman Advanced?

The woman voter would be pernicious to the State not only because she could not back her vote by physical force, but also by reason of her intellectual defects.

Woman's mind attends in appraising a statement primarily to the mental images which it evokes, and only secondarily--and sometimes not at all--to what is predicated in the statement. It is over-influenced by individual instances; arrives at conclusions on incomplete evidence; has a very imperfect sense of proportion; accepts the congenial as true, and rejects the uncongenial as false; takes the imaginary which is desired for reality, and treats the undesired reality which is out of sight as non-existent--building up for itself in this way, when biased by predilections and aversions, a very unreal picture of the external world.

The explanation of this is to be found in all the physiological attachments of woman's mind:[1] in the fact that mental images are in her over-intimately linked up with emotional reflex responses; that yielding to such reflex responses gives gratification; that intellectual analysis and suspense of judgment involve an inhibition of reflex responses which is felt as neural distress; that precipitate judgment brings relief from this physiological strain; and that woman looks upon her mind not as an implement for the pursuit of truth, but as an instrument for providing her with creature comforts in the form of agreeable mental images.

[1] Certain of these have already been referred to in the letter printed in the Appendix (vide p.167 infra).

In order to satisfy the physical yearning for such comforts, a considerable section of intelligent and virtuous women insist on picturing to themselves that the reign of physical force is over, or as good as over; that distinctions based upon physical and intellectual force may be reckoned as non-existent; that male supremacy as resting upon these is a thing of the past; and that Justice means Egalitarian Equity--means equating the weaklings with the strong and the incapable with the capable.

All this because these particular ideas are congenial to the woman of refinement, and because it is to her, when she is a suffragist, uncongenial that there should exist another principle of justice which demands from the physically and intellectually capable that they shall retain the reins of government in their own hands; and specially uncongenial that in all man-governed States the ideas of justice of the more forceful should have worked out so much to the advantage of women, that a large majority of these are indifferent or actively hostile to the Woman's Suffrage Movement.

In further illustration of what has been said above, it may be pointed out that woman, even intelligent woman, nurses all sorts of misconceptions about herself. She, for instance, is constantly picturing to herself that she can as a worker lay claim to the same all-round efficiency as a man--forgetting that woman is notoriously unadapted to tasks in which severe physical hardships have to be confronted; and that hardly any one would, if other alternative offered, employ a woman in any work which imposed upon her a combined physical and mental strain, or in any work where emergencies might have to be faced.

In like manner the suffragist is fond of picturing to herself that woman is for all ordinary purposes the intellectual equal, and that the intelligent woman is the superior of the ordinary man.

These results are arrived at by fixing the attention upon the fact that an ordinary man and an ordinary woman are, from the point of view of memory and apprehension, very much on a level; and that a highly intelligent woman has a quicker memory and a more rapid power of apprehension than the ordinary man; and further, by leaving out of regard that it is not so much a quick memory or a rapid power of apprehension which is required for effective intellectual work, as originality, or at any rate independence of thought, a faculty of felicitious generalisations and diacritical judgment, long-sustained intellectual effort, an unselective mirroring of the world in the mind, and that relative immunity to fallacy which goes together with a stable and comparatively unresponsive nervous system.

When we consider that the intellect of the quite ungifted man works with this last-mentioned physiological advantage, we can see that the male intellect must be, and--pace [with the permission of] the woman suffragist--it in point of fact is, within its range, a better instrument for dealing with the practical affairs of life than that of the intelligent woman.

How far off we are in the case of woman from an unselective mirroring of the world in the mind is shown by the fact that large and important factors of life may be represented in woman's mind by lacunae [gaps] of which she is totally unconscious.

Thus, for instance, that not very unusual type of spinster who is in a condition of retarded development (and you will find this kind of woman even on County Council's), is completely unconscious of the sexual element in herself and in human nature generally. Nay, though one went from the dead, he could not bring it home to her that unsatisfied sexuality is an intellectual disability.

Sufficient illustration will now have been given of woman's incapacity to take a complete or objective view of any matter in which she has a personal, or any kind of emotional interest; and this would now be the place to discuss those other aspects of her mind which are relevant to her claim to the suffrage. I refer to her logical endowment and her political sagacity.

All that I might have been required to say here on these issues has, however, already been said by me in dealing with the arguments of the suffragist. I have there carefully written it in between the lines.

One thing only remains over.--We must, before we pass on, consider whether woman has really, as she tells us, given earnest for the future weeding out of these her secondary sexual characters, by making quite phenomenal advances within the lifetime of the present generation; and, above all, whether there is any basis for woman's confident assurance that, when for a few generations she shall have enjoyed educational advantages, she will at any rate pull up level with man.

The vision of the future may first engage our attention; for only this roseate prospect makes of any man a feminist.

Now the basis that all this hope rests upon is the belief that it is a law of heredity that acquired characteristics are handed down; and, let it be observed, that whereas this theory found, not many decades ago, under the influence of Darwin, thousands of adherents among scientific men, it finds to-day only here and there an adherent.

But let that pass, for we have to consider here, not only whether acquired characteristics are handed down, but further whether, "if we held that doctrine true," it would furnish scientific basis for the belief that educational advantages carried on from generation to generation would level up woman's intellect to man's; and whether, as the suffragist also believes, the narrow education of past generations of women can be held responsible for their present intellectual shortcomings.

A moment's consideration will show--for we may here fix our eyes only on the future--that woman could not hope to advance relatively to man except upon the condition that the acquired characteristics of woman, instead of being handed down equally to her male and female descendants, were accumulated upon her daughters.

Now if that be a law of heredity, it is a law which is as yet unheard of outside the sphere of the woman suffrage societies. Moreover, one is accustomed to hear women, when they are not arguing on the suffrage, allege that clever mothers make clever sons.

It must, as it will have come home to us, be clear to every thoughtful mind that woman's belief that she will, through education and the cumulation of its effects upon her through generations, become a more glorious being, rests, not upon any rational basis, but only on the physiological fact that what is congenial to woman impresses itself upon her as true. All that sober science in the form of history and physiology would seem to entitle us to hope from the future of woman is that she will develop pari passu [step by step] with man; and that education will teach her not to retard him overmuch by her lagging in the rear.

In view of this larger issue, the question as to whether woman has, in any real sense of the word, been making progress in the course of the present generation, loses much of interest.

If to move about more freely, to read more freely, to speak out her mind more freely, and to have emancipated herself from traditionary beliefs--and, I would add, traditionary ethics--is to have advanced, woman has indubitably advanced.

But the educated native too has advanced in all these respects; and he also tells us that he is pulling up level with the white man.

Let us at any rate, when the suffragist is congratulating herself on her own progress, meditate also upon that dictum of Nietzsche, "Progress is writ large on all woman's banners and bannerets; but one can actually see her going back."

III

WOMAN'S DISABILITY IN THE MATTER OF PUBLIC MORALITY

Standards by which Morality can be Appraised--Conflict between Different Moralities--The Correct Standard of Morality--Moral Psychology of Men and Woman--Difference between Man and Woman in Matters of Public Morality.

Yet a third point has to come into consideration in connexion with the woman voter. This is, that she would be pernicious to the State also by virtue of her defective moral equipment.

Let me make clear what is the nature of the defect of morality which is here imputed to woman.

Conduct may be appraised by very different standards.

We may appraise it by reference to a transcendental religious ideal which demands that the physical shall be subordinated to the spiritual, and that the fetters of self should be flung aside.

Or again, we may bring into application purely mundane utilitarian standards, and may account conduct as immoral or moral according as it seeks only the happiness of the agent, or the happiness of the narrow circle of humanity which includes along with him also his relatives and intimate friends, or again, the welfare of the wider circle which includes all those with whom he may have come into contact, or whom he may affect through his work; or again, the welfare of the whole body-politic of which we are members; or lastly, that of the general body of mankind.

Now it might be contended that all these different moralities are in their essence one and the same; and that one cannot comply with the requirements of any one of these systems of morality without fulfilling in a measure the requirements of all the other moralities.

It might, for example, be urged that if a man strive after the achievement of a transcendental ideal in which self shall be annulled, he will pro tanto [to such extent] be bringing welfare to his domestic circle; or again, that it would be impossible to promote domestic welfare without, through this, promoting the welfare of the nation, and through that the general welfare of the world.

In like manner it might be argued that all work done for abstract principles of morality like liberty and justice, for the advancement of knowledge, and for whatever else goes to the building up of a higher civilisation, will, by promoting the welfare of the general body of mankind, redound to the advantage of each several nation, and ultimately to the advantage of each domestic circle.

But all this would be true only in a very superficial and strictly qualified sense. In reality, just as there is eternal conflict between egoism and altruism, so there is conflict between the different moralities.

To take examples, the attempt to actualise the transcendental religious ideal may, when pursued with ardour, very easily conflict with the morality which makes domestic felicity its end. And again--as we see in the anti-militarist movement in France, in the history of the early Christian Church, in the case of the Quakers and in the teachings of Tolstoy--it may quite well set itself in conflict with national ideals, and dictate a line of conduct which is, from the point of view of the State, immoral.

We need no further witness of the divorce between idealistic and national morality than that which is supplied in the memorable utterance of Bishop Magee, "No state which was conducted on truly Christian principles could hold together for a week."

And domestic morality will constantly come into conflict with public morality.

To do everything in one's power to advance one's relatives and friends irrespectively of all considerations of merit would, no doubt, be quite sound domestic morality; it could, however, not always be reconciled with public morality. In the same way, to take one's country's part in all eventualities would be patriotic, but it might quite well conflict with the higher interests of humanity.

Now, the point towards which we have been winning our way is that each man's moral station and degree will be determined by the election which he makes where egoism and altruism, and where a narrower and a wider code of morality, conflict.

That the moral law forbids yielding to the promptings of egoism or to those of the narrower moralities when this involves a violation of the precepts of the wider morality is axiomatic. Criminal and anti-social actions are not excused by the fact that motives which impelled their commission were not purely egoistic.

But the ethical law demands more than abstention from definitely anti-social actions. It demands from every individual that he shall recognise the precepts of public morality as of superior obligation to those of egoism and domestic morality.

By the fact that her public men recognised this ethical law Rome won for herself in the ancient world spectacular grandeur. By an unexampled national obedience to it glory has in our time accrued to Japan. And, in truth, there is not anywhere any honour or renown but such as comes from casting away the bonds of self and of the narrower moralities to carry out the behests of the wider morality.

Even in the strongholds of transcendental religion where it was axiomatic that morality began and was summed up in personal morality, it is gradually coming to be recognised that, where we have two competing moralities, it is always the wider morality which has the prior claim upon our allegiance.

Kingsley's protest against the morality of "saving one's dirty soul" marked a step in advance. And we find full recognition of the superior claim of the larger morality in that other virile dictum of Bishop Magee, "I would rather have England free, than England sober." That is, "I would maintain the conditions which make for the highest civilisation even at the price of a certain number of lapses in personal and domestic morality."

What is here new, let it be noted, is only the acknowledgment by those whose official allegiance is to a transcendental ideal of personal morality that they are called upon to obey a higher allegiance. For there has always existed, in the doctrine that guilty man could not be pardoned and taken back into favour until the claims of eternal justice had been satisfied, theoretical recognition of the principle that one must conform to the precepts of abstract morality before one may ethically indulge oneself in the lower moralities of philanthropy and personal benevolence.

The view point from which I would propose to survey the morality of woman has now been reached. It has, however, still to be pointed out that we may appropriately, in comparing the morals of man and woman, confine our survey to a comparatively narrow field. That is to say, we may here rule out all that relates to purely personal and domestic morality--for this is not relevant to the suffrage. And we may also rule out all that relates to offences against the police laws--such as public drunkenness and offences against the criminal law--for these would come into consideration only in connexion with an absolutely inappreciable fraction of voters.

It will be well to begin by signalising certain points in the moral psychology of man.

When morality takes up its abode in a man who belongs to the intellectual caste it will show itself in his becoming mindful of his public obligations. He will consider the quality of his work as affecting the interest of those who have to place dependence upon it; behaviour to those who are casually brought into relations with him; the discharge of his indebtedness to the community; and the proper conduct of public affairs.

In particular, it will be to him a matter of concern that the law shall be established upon classifications which are just (in the sense of being conformable to public advantage); and that the laws shall everywhere be justly, that is to say rigorously and impartially, administered.

If we now turn to the man in the street we shall not find him especially sensible to the appeals of morality. But when the special call comes it will generally be possible to trust him: as an elector, to vote uninfluenced by considerations of private advantage; and, when called to serve on a jury, to apply legal classifications without distinction of person.

Furthermore, in all times of crisis he may be counted upon to apply the principles of communal morality which have been handed down in the race.

The Titanic disaster, for example, showed in a conspicuous manner that the ordinary man will, "letting his own life go," obey the communal law which lays it upon him, when involved in a catastrophe, to save first the women and children.

Lastly, we come to the man who is intolerant of all the ordinary restraints of personal and domestic morality. Even in him the seeds of communal morality will often be found deeply implanted.

Time and again a regiment of scallawags, who have let all other morality go hang, have, when the proper chord has been made to vibrate in them, heard the call of communal morality, and done deeds which make the ears of whosoever heareth of them to tingle.

We come into an entirely different land when we come to the morality of woman. It is personal and domestic, not public, morality which is instinctive in her.

In other words, when egoism gives ground to altruism, that altruism is exercised towards those who are linked up to her by a bond of sexual affection, or a community in blood, or failing this, by a relation of personal friendship, or by some other personal relation.

And even when altruism has had her perfect work, woman feels no interest in, and no responsibility towards, any abstract moral ideal.

And though the suffragist may protest, instancing in disproof of this her own burning enthusiasm for justice, we, for our part, may legitimately ask whether evidence of a moral enthusiasm for justice would be furnished by a desire to render to others their due, or by vehement insistence upon one's own rights, and systematic attempts to extort, under the cover of the word "justice," advantages for oneself.

But it will be well to dwell a little longer on, and to bring out more clearly, the point that woman's moral ideals are personal and domestic, as distinguished from impersonal and public.

Let us note in this connexion that it would be difficult to conceive of a woman who had become deaf to the appeal of personal and domestic morality making it a matter of amour propre to respond to a call of public morality; and difficult to conceive of a woman recovering lost self-respect by fulfilling such an obligation.

But one knows that woman will rise and respond to the call of any strong human or transcendental personal affection.

Again, it is only a very exceptional woman who would, when put to her election between the claims of a narrow and domestic and a wider or public morality, subordinate the former to the latter.

In ordinary life, at any rate, one finds her following in such a case the suggestions of domestic--I had almost called it animal--morality.

It would be difficult to find any one who would trust a woman to be just to the rights of others in the case where the material interests of her children, or of a devoted husband, were involved. And even to consider the question of being in such a case intellectually just to any one who came into competition with personal belongings like husband and child would, of course, lie quite beyond the moral horizon of ordinary woman.

It is not only the fact that the ideals of abstract justice and truth would inevitably be brushed aside by woman in the interests of those she loves which comes into consideration here; it is also the fact that woman is almost without a moral sense in the matter of executing a public trust such as voting or attaching herself to a political association with a view to influencing votes.

There is between man and woman here a characteristic difference.

While it is, of course, not a secret to anybody that the baser sort of man can at any time be diverted from the path of public morality by a monetary bribe or other personal advantage, he will not, at any rate, set at naught all public morality by doing so for a peppercorn. He will, for instance, not join, for the sake of a daughter, a political movement in which he has no belief; nor vote for this or that candidate just to please a son; or censure a member of Parliament who has in voting on female suffrage failed to consider the predilections of his wife.

But woman, whether she be politically enfranchised as in Australasia, or unenfranchised as at home; whether she be immoral in the sense of being purely egoistic, or moral in the sense of being altruistic, very rarely makes any secret or any shame of doing these things.

In this matter one would not be very far from the truth if one alleged that there are no good women, but only women who have lived under the influence of good men.

Even more serious than this postponement of public to private morality is the fact that even reputedly ethical women will, in the interests of what they take to be idealistic causes, violate laws which are universally accepted as being of moral obligation.

I here pass over the recent epidemic of political crime among women to advert to the want of conscience which permits, in connexion with professedly idealistic causes, not only misrepresentations, but the making of deliberately false statements on matters of public concern.

It is, for example, an illustration of the profoundly different moral atmospheres in which men and women live that when a public woman recently made, for what was to her an idealistic purpose, a deliberately false statement of fact in The Times, she quite naively confessed to it, seeing nothing whatever amiss in her action.

And it did not appear that any other woman suffragist could discern any kind of immorality in it. The worst thing they could find to say was that it perhaps was a little gauche to confess to making a deliberately false statement on a public question when it was for the moment particularly desirable that woman should show up to best advantage before the eyes of man.

We may now for a moment put aside the question of woman's public morality and consider a question which is inextricably mixed up with the question of the admission of woman to the suffrage. This is the mental attitude and the programme of the female legislative reformer.

IV

MENTAL OUTLOOK AND PROGRAMME OF THE FEMALE LEGISLATIVE REFORMER

The suffragist woman, when she is the kind of woman who piques herself upon her ethical impulses, will, even when she is intellectually very poorly equipped, and there is no imprint of altruism upon her life, assure you that nothing except the moral influence of woman, exerted through the legislation, which her practical mind would be capable of initiating, will ever avail to abate existing social evils, and to effect the moral redemption of the world.

It will not be amiss first to try to introduce a little clearness and order into our ideas upon those formidably difficult problems which the female legislative reformer desires to attack, and then to consider how a rational reforming mind would go to work in the matter of proposing legislation for these.

First would come those evils which result from individuals seeking advantage to themselves by the direct infliction of injury upon others. Violations of the criminal law and the various forms of sweating and fleecing one's fellow-men come under this category.

Then would come the evils which arise out of purveying physiological and psychological refreshments and excitements, which are, according as they are indulged in temperately or intemperately, grateful and innocuous, or sources of disaster and ruin. The evils which are associated with the drink traffic and the betting industry are typical examples.

Finally, there would come into consideration the evils of death or physical suffering deliberately inflicted by man upon man with a view to preventing worse evils. The evil of war would come under this category. In this same category might also come the much lesser evil of punitive measures inflicted upon criminals. And with this might be coupled the evil of killing and inflicting physical suffering upon animals for the advantage of man.

We may now consider how the rational legislative reformer would in each case go to work.

He would not start with the assumption that it must be possible by some alteration of the law to abolish or conspicuously reduce any of the afore-mentioned evils; nor yet with the assumption that, if a particular alteration of the law would avail to bring about this result, that alteration ought necessarily to be made. He would recognise that many things which are theoretically desirable are unattainable; and that many legislative measures which could perfectly well be enforced would be barred by the fact that they would entail deplorable unintended consequences.

The rational legislator whom we have here in view would accordingly always take expert advice as to whether the desired object could be achieved by legal compulsion; and as to whether a projected law which satisfied the condition of being workable would give a balance of advantages over disadvantages.

In connexion with a proposal for the prevention of sweating he would, for instance, take expert advice as to whether its provisions could be enforced; and whether, if enforceable, they would impose added hardships on any class of employees or penalties on any innocent class of employers.

In like manner in connexion with a proposed modification in criminal procedure, the rational reformer would defer to the expert on the question as to whether such modification would secure greater certainty of punishment for the guilty without increasing the risk of convicting the innocent.

In connexion with the second category of evils--the category under which would come those of drinking and betting--the rational legislative reformer would recognise the complete impracticability of abolishing by legislative prohibition physiological indulgences and the evils which sometimes attend upon them.

He would consider instead whether these attendant evils could be reduced by making the regulating laws more stringent; and whether more stringent restrictions--in addition to the fact that they would filch from the all too small stock of human happiness--would not, by paving the way for further invasions of personal liberty, cripple the free development of the community.

On the former question, which only experts could properly answer, the reasonable reformer would defer to their advice. The answer to the last question he would think out for himself.

In connexion with the evils which are deliberately inflicted by man with a view to reaping either personal profit, or profit for the nation, or profit for humanity, the reasonable reformer would begin by making clear to himself that the world we live in is not such a world as idealism might conjure up, but a world of violence, in which life must be taken and physical suffering be inflicted.

And he would recognise that the vital material interests of the nation can be protected only by armed force; that civilisation can be safeguarded only by punishing violations of the criminal law; and that the taking of animal life and the infliction of a certain amount of physical suffering upon animals is essential to human well-being, comfort, and recreation; and essential also to the achievement of the knowledge which is required to combat disease.

And the reasonable reformer will, in conformity with this, direct his efforts, not to the total abolition of war, but to the prevention of such wars as are not waged for really vital material interests, and to the abatement of the ferocities of warfare.

In the case of punishment for criminals he would similarly devote his efforts not to the abrogation of punishments, but to the relinquishment of any that are not reformatory, or really deterrent.

In like manner the reasonable reformer would not seek to prohibit the slaughtering of animals for food, or the killing off of animal pests, or the trapping, shooting, or hunting of animals for sport or profit, nor yet would he seek to prevent their utilisation of animals for the acquirement of knowledge.

He would direct his efforts to reducing the pain which is inflicted, and to preserving everywhere measure and scale--not sentimentally forbidding in connexion with one form of utilisation of animals what is freely allowed in connexion with another--but differentiating, if differentiating at all in favour of permitting the infliction of proportionately greater suffering in the case where national and humanitarian interests, than in the case where mere recreation and luxury and personal profit, are at stake.

Having recognised what reason would prescribe to the legislative reformer, we have next to inquire how far the man voter conforms to these prescriptions of reason, and how far the woman reformer would do so if she became a voter.

Let it be noted that the man in the street makes no question about falling in with the fact that he is born into a world of violence, and he acquiesces in the principle that the State, and, failing the State, the individual, may employ force and take life in defence of vital material interests. And he frankly falls in with it being a matter of daily routine to kill and inflict suffering upon animals for human profit or advantage.

Even if these principles are not formulated by the man in the street in quite such plain terms, he not only carries them out in practice, but he conducts all his thinking upon these presuppositions.

He, for instance, would fall in with the proposition that morality does not require from man that he should give up taking life or inflicting physical suffering. And he would not cavil with the statement that man should put reasonable limits to the amount of suffering he inflicts, and confine this within as narrow a range as possible--always requiring for the death or suffering inflicted some tangible advantage.

Moreover, if the question should be raised as to whether such advantage will result, the ordinary man will as a rule, where the matter lies beyond his personal ken, take expert opinion before intervening.

He will, for instance, be prepared to be so guided in connexion with such questions as whether disease could, if more knowledge were available, be to a large extent prevented and cured; as to how far animal experiments would contribute to the acquirement of that knowledge; and as to how far the physical suffering which might be involved in these experiments can be minimised or abolished. But not every man is prepared to fall in with this programme of inflicting physical suffering for the relief of physical suffering. There is also a type of spiritually-minded man who in this world of violence sets his face uncompromisingly against the taking of any life and the infliction of any physical suffering--refusing to make himself a partaker of evil.

An idealist of this type will, like Tolstoy, be an anti-militarist. He will advocate a general gaol delivery for criminals. He will be a vegetarian. He will not allow an animal's life to be taken in his house, though the mice scamper over his floors. And he will, consistently with his conviction that it is immoral to resort to force, refuse to take any part in legislation or government.

This attitude, which is that commended by the Hindoo and the Buddhist religions, is, of course, a quite unpractical attitude towards life. It is, in fact, a self-destructive attitude, unless a man's fellow-citizens are prepared by forcible means to secure to him the enjoyment of the work of his hands or of his inherited property, or unless those who refuse to desist from the exercise of force are prepared to untake the support of idealists.

We have not only these two classes of men--the ordinary man who has no compunction in resorting to force when the requirements of life demand it, and the idealist who refuses to have any lot or part in violence; there is also a hybrid. This male hybrid will descant on the general iniquity of violence, and then not only connive at those forms of violence which minister to his personal comforts, but also make a virtue of trying to abate by legal violence some particular form of physical suffering which happens to offend in a quite special manner his individual sensibility.

There is absolutely nothing to be said about this kind of reforming crank, except only that anything which may be said in relation to the female legislative reformer may be appositely said of him; and perhaps also this, that the ordinary man holds him both in intellectual and in moral contempt, and is resolved not to allow him to do any really serious injury to the community.

To become formidable this quasi-male person must, as he recognises, ally himself with the female legislative reformer.

Passing on to deal with her, it imports us first to realise that while the male voter has--except where important constitutional issues were in question--been accustomed to leave actual legislation to the expert, the female reformer gives notice beforehand that she will, as soon as ever she gets the suffrage, insist on pressing forward by her vote her reforming schemes.

What would result from the ordinary voter legislating on matters which require expert knowledge will be plain to every one who will consider the evolution of law.

There stand over against each other here, as an example and a warning, the Roman Law, which was the creation of legal experts: the praetor and the jurisconsult; and the legal system of the Greeks, which was the creation of a popular assembly--and it was a popular assembly which was quite ideally intelligent.

Upon the Roman Law has been built the law of the greater part of the civilised world. The Greek is a by-word for inconsequence.

How can one, then, without cold shudders think of that legal system which the female amateur legal reformer would bring to the birth?

Let us consider her qualifications. Let us first take cognisance of the fact that the reforming woman will neither stand to the principle that man may, where this gives a balance of advantage, inflict on his fellow-man, and a fortiori upon animals, death and physical suffering; nor yet will she stand to the principle that it is ethically unlawful to do deeds of violence.

She spends her life halting between these two opinions, eternally shilly-shallying.

She will, for instance, begin by announcing that it can never be lawful to do evil that good may come; and that killing and inflicting suffering is an evil. (In reality the precept of not doing evil that good may come has relation only to breaking for idealistic purposes moral laws of higher obligation.) She will then go back upon that and concede that war may sometimes be lawful, and that the punishment of criminals is not an evil. But if her emotions are touched by the forcible feeding of a criminal militant suffragist, she will again go back upon that and declare that the application of force is an intolerable evil.

Or, again, she will concede that the slaughtering of animals for food is not an evil, but that what is really unforgivable is the infliction of physical suffering on animals. And all the time for her, as well as for man, calves and lambs are being emasculated to make her meat succulent; wild animals are painfully done to death to provide her table with delicacies; birds with young in the nest are shot so that she may parade in their plumage; or fur-bearing animals are for her comfort and adornment massacred and tortured in traps.

When a man crank who is co-responsible for these things begins to talk idealistic reforms, the ordinary decent man refuses to have anything more to say to him.

But when a woman crank holds this language, the man merely shrugs his shoulders. "It is," he tells himself, "after all, the woman whom God gave him."

It must be confessed that the problem as to how man with a dual nature may best accommodate himself to a world of violence presents a very difficult problem.

It would obviously be no solution to follow out everywhere a programme of violence. Not even the predatory animals do that. Tigers do not savage their cubs; hawks do not pluck hawks' eyes; and dogs do not fight bitches.

Nor would, as has been shown, the solution of the problem be arrived at by everywhere surrendering--if we had been given the grace to do this--to the compunctious visitings of nature.

What is required is to find the proper compromise. As to what that would be there is, as between the ordinary man and woman on the one side, and the male crank and the battalions of sentimental women on the other, a conflict which is, to all intents and purposes, a sex war.

The compromise which ordinary human nature had fixed upon--and it is one which, ministering as it does to the survival of the race, has been adopted through the whole range of nature--is that of making within the world in which violence rules a series of enclaves in which the application of violence is progressively restricted and limited.

Outside the outermost of the series of ring fences thus constituted would be the realm of uncompromising violence such as exists when human life is endangered by wild animals, or murderous criminals, or savages. Just within this outermost fence would be civilised war--for in civilised war non-combatants and prisoners and wounded are excluded from the application of violence. In like manner we bring humanity in general within a more sheltered enclosure than animals--pet animals within a more sheltered enclosure than other animals. Again, we bring those who belong to the white race within a narrower protecting circle than mankind in general, and those of our own nation within a still narrower one.

Following out the same principle, we include women and children within a narrower shelter fence than our adult fellow-male; and we use the weapon of force more reluctantly when we are dealing with our relatives and friends than when we are dealing with those who are not personally known to us; and finally, we lay it aside more completely when we are dealing with the women of our households than when we are dealing with the males.

The cause of civilisation and of the amenities, and the welfare of the nation, of the family, and of woman, are all intimately bound up with a faithful adherence to this compromise.

But this policy imposes upon those whom it shelters from violence corresponding obligations.

In war non-combatants--not to speak of the wounded on the battlefield--must desist from hostile action on the pain of being shot down like wild beasts. And though an individual non-combatant might think it a patriotic action for him to take part in war, the thoughtful man would recognise that such action was a violation of a well-understood covenant made in the interest of civilisation, and that to break through this covenant was to abrogate a humanitarian arrangement by which the general body of non-combatants immensely benefits.

Exactly the same principle finds, as already pointed out, application when a woman employs direct violence, or aspires to exercise by voting indirect violence.

One always wonders if the suffragist appreciates all that woman stands to lose and all that she imperils by resort to physical force. One ought not to have to tell her that, if she had to fight for her position, her status would be that which is assigned to her among the Kaffirs--not that which civilised man concedes to her.

>From considering the compromise by which man adapts his dual nature to violence in the world, we turn to that which the female legislative reformer would seek to impose by the aid of her vote.

Her proposal, as the reader will have discerned, would be that all those evils which make appeal to the feminine emotions should be legally prohibited, and that all those which fail to make this appeal shall be tolerated.

In the former class would be included those which come directly under woman's ken, or have been brought vividly before the eyes of her imagination by emotional description. And the specially intolerable evils will be those which, owing to the fact that they fall upon woman or her immediate belongings, induce in the female legislative reformer pangs of sympathetic discomfort.

In the class of evils which the suffragist is content to tolerate, or say nothing about, would be those which are incapable of evoking in her such sympathetic pangs, and she concerns herself very little with those evils which do not furnish her with a text for recriminations against man.

Conspicuous in this programme is the absence of any sense of proportion. One would have imagined that it would have been plain to everybody that the evils which individual women suffer at the hands of man are very far from being the most serious ills of humanity. One would have imagined that the suffering inflicted by disease and by bad social conditions--suffering which falls upon man and woman alike--deserved a first place in the thoughts of every reformer. And one might have expected it to be common knowledge that the wrongs individual men inflict upon women have a full counterpart in the wrongs which individual women inflict upon men. It may quite well be that there are mists which here "blot and fill the perspective" of the female legislative reformer. But to look only upon one's own things, and not also upon the things of others, is not for that morally innocent.

There is further to be noted in connexion with the female legislative reformer that she has never been able to see why she should be required to put her aspirations into practical shape, or to consider ways and means, or to submit the practicability of her schemes to expert opinion. One also recognises that from a purely human point of view such tactics are judicious. For if the schemes of the female legislative reformer were once to be reviewed from the point of view of their practicability, her utility as a legislator would come into question, and the suffragist could no longer give out that there has been committed to her from on High a mission to draw water for man-kind out of the wells of salvation.

Lastly, we have to reflect in connection with the female legislative reformer that to go about proposing to reform the laws means to abandon that special field of usefulness which lies open to woman in alleviating misery and redressing those hard cases which will, under all laws and regulations of human manufacture and under all social dispositions, inevitably occur. Now when a woman leaves a social task which is commensurate with her abilities, and which asks from her personal effort and self-sacrifice, for a task which is quite beyond her abilities, but which, she thinks, will bring her personal kudos, shall we impute it to her for righteousness?

V

ULTERIOR ENDS WHICH THE WOMAN'S SUFFRAGE MOVEMENT HAS IN VIEW

We have now sufficiently considered the suffragist's humanitarian schemes, and we may lead up to the consideration of her further projects by contrasting woman's suffrage as it presents itself under colonial conditions-- i.e. woman's suffrage without the female legislative reformer and the feminist--with the woman suffrage which is being agitated for in England--i.e. woman suffrage with the female legislative reformer and the feminist.

In the colonies and undeveloped countries generally where women are in a minority, and where owing to the fact that practically all have an opportunity of marrying, there are not for woman any difficult economic and physiological conditions, there is no woman's question; and by consequence no female legislative reformer or feminist. The woman voter follows, as the opportunist politicians who enfranchised her intended, the lead of her men-folk--serving only a pawn in the game of politics. Under such conditions woman's suffrage kleaves things as they are, except only that it undermines the logical foundations of the law, and still further debases the standard of public efficiency and public morality.

In countries, such as England, where an excess female population [1] has made economic difficulties for woman, and where the severe sexual restrictions, which here obtains, have bred in her sex-hostility, the suffrage movement has as its avowed ulterior object the abrogation of all distinctions which depend upon sex; and the achievement of the economic independence of woman.

[1] In England and Wales there are, in a population of 8,000,000 women between the ages of twenty and fifty, 3,000,000 unmarried women.

To secure this economic independence every post, occupation, and Government service is to be thrown open to woman; she is to receive everywhere the same wages as man; male and female are to work side by side; and they are indiscriminately to be put in command the one over the other. Furthermore, legal rights are to be secured to the wife over her husband's property and earnings. The programme is, in fact, to give to woman an economic independence out of the earnings and taxes of man.

Nor does feminist ambition stop short here. It demands that women shall be included in every advisory committee, every governing board, every jury, every judicial bench, every electorate, every parliament, and every ministerial cabinet; further, that every masculine foundation, university, school of learning, academy, trade union, professional corporation and scientific society shall be converted into an epicene institution--until we shall have everywhere one vast cock-and-hen show.

The proposal to bring man and woman together everywhere into extremely intimate relationships raises very grave questions. It brings up, first, the question of sexual complications; secondly, the question as to whether the tradition of modesty and reticence between the sexes is to be definitely sacrificed; and, most important of all, the question as to whether epicene conditions would place obstacles in the way of intellectual work.

Of these issues the feminist puts the first two quite out of account. I have already elsewhere said my say upon these matters.[1] With regard to the third, the feminist either fails to realise that purely intellectual intercourse--as distinguished from an intercommunion of mental images--with woman is to a large section of men repugnant; or else, perceiving this, she makes up her mind that, this notwithstanding, she will get her way by denouncing the man who does not welcome her as selfish; and by insisting that under feminism (the quotation is from Mill, the italics which question his sincerity are mine) "the mass of mental faculties available for the higher service of mankind would be doubled."

[1] Vide Appendix, pp. 169-173.

The matter cannot so lightly be disposed of. It will be necessary for us to find out whether really intimate association with woman on the purely intellectual plane is realisable. And if it is, in fact, unrealisable, it will be necessary to consider whether it is the exclusion of women from masculine corporations; or the perpetual attempt of women to force their way into these, which would deserve to be characterised as selfish.

In connexion with the former of these issues, we have to consider here not whether that form of intellectual co-operation in which the man plays the game, and the woman moves the pawns under his orders, is possible. That form of co-operation is of course possible, and it has, doubtless, certain utilities.

Nor yet have we to consider whether quite intimate and purely intellectual association on an equal footing between a particular man and a selected woman may or may not be possible. It will suffice to note that the feminist alleges that this also is possible; but everybody knows that the woman very often marries the man.

What we have to ask is whether--even if we leave out of regard the whole system of attractions or, as the case may be, repulsions which come into operation when the sexes are thrown together--purely intellectual intercourse between man and the typical unselected woman is not barred by the intellectual immoralities and limitations which appear to be secondary sexual characters of woman.

With regard to this issue, there would seem to be very little real difference of opinion among men. But there are great differences in the matter of candour. There are men who speak out, and who enunciate like Nietzsche that "man and woman are alien--never yet has any one conceived how alien."

There are men who, from motives of delicacy or policy, do not speak out-- averse to saying anything that might be unflattering to woman.

And there are men who are by their profession of the feminist faith debarred from speaking out, but who upon occasion give themselves away.

Of such is the man who in the House of Commons champions the cause of woman's suffrage, impassionately appealing to Justice; and then betrays himself by announcing that he would shake off from his feet the dust of its purlieus if ever women were admitted as members--i.e. if ever women were forced upon him as close intellectual associates.

Wherever we look we find aversion to compulsory intellectual co-operation with woman. We see it in the sullen attitude which the ordinary male student takes up towards the presence of women students in his classes. We see it in the fact that the older English universities, which have conceded everything else to women, have made a strong stand against making them actual members of the university; for this would impose them on men as intellectual associates. Again we see the aversion in the opposition to the admission of women to the bar. But we need not look so far afield. Practically every man feels that there is in woman--patent, or hidden away--an element of unreason which, when you come upon it, summarily puts an end to purely intellectual intercourse. One may reflect, for example, upon the way the woman's suffrage controversy has been conducted.

Proceeding now on the assumption that these things are so, and that man feels that he and woman belong to different intellectual castes, we come now to the question as to whether it is man who is selfish when he excludes women from his institutions, or woman when she unceasingly importunes for admittance. And we may define as selfish all such conduct as pursues the advantage of the agent at the cost of the happiness and welfare of the general body of mankind.

We shall be in a better position to pronounce judgment on this question of ethics when we have considered the following series of analogies:

When a group of earnest and devout believers meet together for special intercession and worship, we do not tax them with selfishness if they exclude unbelievers.

Nor do we call people who are really devoted to music selfish if, coming together for this, they make a special point of excluding the unmusical.

Nor again would the imputation of selfishness lie against members of a club for black-balling a candidate who would, they feel, be uncongenial.

Nor should we regard it as an act of selfishness if the members of a family circle, or of the same nation, or of any social circle, desired to come together quite by themselves.

Nor yet would the term selfish apply to an East End music hall audience when they eject any one who belongs to a different social class to themselves and wears good clothes.

And the like would hold true of servants resenting their employers intruding upon them in their hours of leisure or entertainments.

If we do not characterise such exclusions as selfish, but rather respect and sympathise with them, it is because we recognise that the whole object and raison d' etre of association would in each case be nullified by the weak-minded admission of the incompatible intruder.

We recognise that if any charge of selfishness would lie, it would lie against that intruder.

Now if this holds in the case where the interests of religious worship or music, or family, national, or social life, or recreation and relaxation after labour are in question, it will hold true even more emphatically where the interests of intellectual work are involved.

But the feminist will want to argue. She will--taking it as always for granted that woman has a right to all that men's hands or brains have fashioned--argue that it is very important for the intellectual development of woman that she should have exactly the same opportunities as man. And she will, scouting [rejecting with contempt] the idea of any differences between the intelligences of man and woman, discourse to you of their intimate affinity.

It will, perhaps, be well to clear up these points.

The importance of the higher development of woman is unquestionable.

But after all it is the intellect of man which really comes into account in connexion with "the mass of mental faculties available for the higher service of mankind."

The maintenance of the conditions which allow of man's doing his best intellectual work is therefore an interest which is superior to that of the intellectual development of woman. And woman might quite properly be referred for her intellectual development to instructional institutions which should be special to herself.

Coming to the question of the intimate resemblances between the masculine and the feminine intelligence, no man would be venturesome enough to dispute these, but he may be pardoned if he thinks--one would hope in no spirit of exaltation--also of the differences.

We have an instructive analogy in connexion with the learned societies.

It is uncontrovertible that every candidate for election into such a society will have, and will feel that he has, affinities with the members of that association. And he is invited to set these forth in his application. But there may also be differences of which he is not sensible. On that question the electors are the judges; and they are the final court of appeal.

There would seem to be here a moral which the feminist would do well to lay to heart.

There is also another lesson which she might very profitably consider. A quite small difference will often constitute as effective a bar to a useful and congenial co-operation as a more fundamental difference.

In the case of a body of intellectual workers one might at first sight suppose that so small a distinction as that of belonging to a different nationality--sex, of course, is an infinitely profounder difference--would not be a bar to unrestricted intellectual co-operation.

But in point of fact it is in every country, in every learned society, a uniform rule that when foreign scientists or scholars are admitted they are placed not on the ordinary list of working members, but on a special list.

One discerns that there is justification for this in the fact that a foreigner would in certain eventualities be an incompatible person.

One may think of the eventuality of the learned society deciding to recognise a national service, or to take part in a national movement. And one is not sure that a foreigner might not be an incompatible person in the eventuality of a scientist or scholar belonging to a nationality with which the foreigner's country was at feud being brought forward for election. And he would, of course, be an impossible person in a society if he were, in a spirit of chauvinism, to press for a larger representation of his own fellow-countrymen.

Now this is precisely the kind of way man feels about woman. He recognises that she is by virtue of her sex for certain purposes an incompatible person; and that, quite apart from this, her secondary sexual characters might in certain eventualities make her an impossible person.

We may note, before passing on, that these considerations would seem to prescribe that woman should be admitted to masculine institutions only when real humanitarian grounds demand it; that she should--following here the analogy of what is done in the learned societies with respect to foreigners--be invited to co-operate with men only when she is quite specially eminent, or beyond all question useful for the particular purpose in hand; and lastly, that when co-opted into any masculine institution woman should always be placed upon a special list, to show that it was proposed to confine her co-operation within certain specified limits.

>From these general questions, which affect only the woman with intellectual aspirations, we pass to consider what would be the effect of feminism upon the rank and file of women if it made of these co-partners with man in work. They would suffer not only because woman's physiological disabilities and the restrictions which arise out of her sex place her at a great disadvantage when she has to enter into competition with man, but also because under feminism man would be less and less disposed to take off woman's shoulders a part of her burden.

And there can be no dispute that the most valuable financial asset of the ordinary woman is the possibility that a man may be willing--and may, if only woman is disposed to fulfil her part of the bargain, be not only willing but anxious--to support her and to secure for her, if he can, a measure of that freedom which comes from the possession of money.

In view of this every one who has a real fellow-feeling for woman, and who is concerned for her material welfare, as a father is concerned for his daughter's, will above everything else desire to nurture and encourage in man the sentiment of chivalry, and in woman that disposition of mind that makes chivalry possible.

And the woman workers who have to fight the battle of life for themselves would indirectly profit from this fostering of chivalry; for those women who are supported by men do not compete in the limited labour market which is open to the woman worker.

>From every point of view, therefore, except perhaps that of the exceptional woman who would be able to hold her own against masculine competition--and men always issue informal letters of naturalisation to such an exceptional woman--the woman suffrage which leads up to feminism would be a social disaster.

PART III

IS THERE, IF THE SUFFRAGE IS BARRED, ANY PALLIATIVE OF CORRECTIVE FOR

THE DISCONTENTS OF WOMAN?

I

PALLIATIVES OR CORRECTIVES FOR THE DISCONTENTS OF WOMAN

What are the Suffragist's Grievances?--Economic and Physiological Difficulties of Woman--Intellectual Grievances of Suffragist and Corrective.

Is there then, let us ask ourselves, if the suffrage with its programme of feminism is barred as leading to social disaster, any palliative or corrective that can be applied to the present discontents of woman?

If such is to be found, it is to be found only by placing clearly before us the suffragist's grievances.

These grievances are, first, the economic difficulties of the woman who seeks to earn her living by work other than unskilled manual labour; secondly, the difficult physiological conditions in which woman is placed by the excess of the female over the male population and by her diminished chances of marriage [1]; and thirdly, the tedium which obsesses the life of the woman who is not forced, and cannot force herself, to work. On the top of these grievances comes the fact that the suffragist conceives herself to be harshly and unfairly treated by man. This last is the fire which sets a light to all the inflammable material.

[1] Vide footnote, p. 138.

It would be quite out of question to discuss here the economic and physiological difficulties of woman. Only this may be said: it is impossible, in view of the procession of starved and frustrated lives which is continuously filing past, to close one's eyes to the urgency of this woman's problem.

After all, the primary object of all civilisation is to provide for every member of the community food and shelter and fulfilment of natural cravings. And when, in what passes as a civilised community, a whole class is called upon to go without any one of these our human requirements, it is little wonder that it should break out.

But when a way of escape stands open revolt is not morally justified.

Thus, for example, a man who is born into, but cannot support himself in, a superior class of society is not, as long as he can find a livelihood abroad in a humbler walk in life, entitled to revolt.

No more is the woman who is in economic or physiological difficulties. For, if only she has the pluck to take it, a way of escape stands open to her.

She can emigrate; she can go out from the social class in which she is not self-supporting into a humbler social class in which she could earn a living; and she can forsake conditions in which she must remain a spinster for conditions in which she may perhaps become a mother. Only in this way can the problem of finding work, and relief of tedium, for the woman who now goes idle be resolved.

If women were to avail themselves of these ways of escape out of unphysiological conditions, the woman agitator would probably find it as difficult to keep alive a passionate agitation for woman suffrage as the Irish Nationalist agitator to keep alive, after the settlement of the land question and the grant of old age pensions, a passionate agitation for a separate Parliament for Ireland.

For the happy wife and mother is never passionately concerned about the suffrage. It is always the woman who is galled either by physiological hardships, or by the fact that she has not the same amount of money as man, or by the fact that man does not desire her as a co-partner in work, and withholds the homage which she thinks he ought to pay to her intellect.

For this class of grievances the present education of woman is responsible. The girl who is growing up to woman's estate is never taught where she stands relatively to man. She is not taught anything about woman's physical disabilities. She is not told--she is left to discover it for herself when too late-- that child and husband are to woman physiological requirements. She is not taught the defects and limitations of the feminine mind. One might almost think there were no such defects and limitations; and that woman was not always overestimating her intellectual power. And the ordinary girl is not made to realise woman's intrinsically inferior money-earning capacity. She is not made to realise that the woman who cannot work with her hands is generally hard put to earn enough to keep herself alive in the incomplete condition of a spinster.

As a result of such education, when, influenced by the feminist movement, woman comes to institute a comparison between herself and man, she brings into that comparison all those qualities in which she is substantially his equal, and leaves out of account all those in which she is his inferior.

The failure to recognise that man is the master, and why he is the master, lies at the root of the suffrage movement. By disregarding man's superior physical force, the power of compulsion upon which all government is based is disregarded. By leaving out of account those powers of the mind in which man is the superior, woman falls into the error of thinking that she can really compete with him, and that she belongs to the self-same intellectual caste. Finally, by putting out of sight man's superior money-earning capacity, the power of the purse is ignored.

Uninstructed woman commits also another fundamental error in her comparison. Instead of comparing together the average man and the average woman, she sets herself to establish that there is no defect in woman which cannot be discovered also in man; and that there is no virtue or power in the ordinary man which cannot be discovered also in woman. Which having been established to her satisfaction, she is led inevitably to the conclusion that there is nothing whatever to choose between the sexes. And from this there is only a step to the position that human beings ought to be assigned, without distinction of sex, to each and every function which would come within the range of their individual capacities, instead of being assigned as they are at present: men to one function, and women to another.

Here again women ought to have been safeguarded by education. She ought to have been taught that even when an individual woman comes up to the average of man this does not abrogate the disqualification which attaches to a difference of sex. Nor yet--as every one who recognises that we live in a world which conducts itself by generalisations will see--does it abrogate the disqualification of belonging to an inferior intellectual caste.

The present system of feminine education is blameworthy not only in the respect that it fails to draw attention to these disqualifications and to teach woman where she stands; it is even more blameworthy in that it fails to convey to the girl who is growing up any conception of that absolutely elementary form of morality which consists in distinguishing meum and tuum [that which is mine and _that which is yours_].

Instead of her educators encouraging every girl to assert "rights" as against man, and put forward claims, they ought to teach her with respect to him those lessons of behaviour which are driven home once for all into every boy at a public school.

Just as there you learn that you may not make unwarranted demands upon your fellow, and just as in the larger world every nation has got to learn that it cannot with impunity lay claim to the possessions of its neighbours, so woman will have to learn that when things are not offered to her, and she has not the power to take them by force, she has got to make the best of things as they are.

One would wish for every girl who is growing up to womanhood that it might be brought home to her by some refined and ethically-minded member of her own sex how insufferable a person woman becomes when, like a spoilt child, she exploits the indulgence of man; when she proclaims that it is his duty to serve her and to share with her his power and possessions; when she makes an outcry when he refuses to part with what is his own; and when she insists upon thrusting her society upon men everywhere.

And every girl ought to be warned that to embark upon a policy of recrimination when you do not get what you want, and to proclaim yourself a martyr when, having hit, you are hit back, is the way to get yourself thoroughly disliked.

Finally, every girl ought to be shown, in the example of the militant suffragist, how revolt and martyrdom, undertaken in order to possess oneself of what belongs to others, effects the complete disorganisation of moral character.

No one would wish that in the education of girls these quite unlovely things should be insisted upon more than was absolutely necessary. But one would wish that the educators of the rising generation of women should, basing themselves upon these foundations, point out to every girl how great is woman's debt to civilisation; in other words, how much is under civilisation done for woman by man.

And one would wish that, in a world which is rendered unwholesome by feminism, every girl's eyes were opened to comprehend the great outstanding fact of the world: the fact that, turn where you will, you find individual man showering upon individual woman--one man in tribute to her enchantment, another out of a sense of gratitude, and another just because she is something that is his--every good thing which, suffrage or no suffrage, she never could have procured for herself.

APPENDIX

LETTER ON MILITANT HYSTERIA

Reprinted by permission from The Times (London), March 28, 1912.

TO THE EDITOR OF THE TIMES

SIR,--For man the physiological psychology of woman is full of difficulties.

He is not a little mystified when he encounters in her periodically recurring phases of hypersensitiveness, unreasonableness, and loss of the sense of proportion.

He is frankly perplexed when confronted with a complete alteration of character in a woman who is child-bearing.

When he is a witness of the "tendency of woman to morally warp when nervously ill," and of the terrible physical havoc which the pangs of a disappointed love may work, he is appalled.

And it leaves on his mind an eerie feeling when he sees serious and long-continued mental disorders developing in connexion with the approaching extinction of a woman's reproductive faculty.

No man can close his eyes to these things; but he does not feel at liberty to speak of them.

"For the woman that God gave him is not his to give away."[1]

[1 From "The Female of the Species" by Rudyard Kipling]

As for woman herself, she makes very light of any of these mental upsettings.

She perhaps smiles a little at them. . . .[1]

[1] In the interests of those who feel that female dignity is compromised by it, I have here omitted a woman's flippant overestimate of the number of women in London society who suffer from nervous disorders at the climacteric [i.e. menopause].

None the less, these upsettings of her mental equilibrium are the things that a woman has most cause to fear; and no doctor can ever lose sight of the fact that the mind of woman is always threatened with danger from the reverberations of her physiological emergencies.

It is with such thoughts that the doctor lets his eyes rest upon the militant suffragist. He cannot shut them to the fact that there is mixed up with the woman's movement much mental disorder; and he cannot conceal from himself the physiological emergencies which lie behind.

The recruiting field for the militant suffragists is the million of our excess female population--that million which had better long ago have gone out to mate with its complement of men beyond the sea.

Among them there are the following different types of women:--

(a) First--let us put them first--come a class of women who hold, with minds otherwise unwarped, that they may, whenever it is to their advantage, lawfully resort to physical violence.

The programme, as distinguished from the methods, of these women is not very different from that of the ordinary suffragist woman.

(b) There file past next a class of women who have all their life-long been strangers to joy, women in whom instincts long suppressed have in the end broken into flame. These are the sexually embittered women in whom everything has turned into gall and bitterness of heart, and hatred of men.

Their legislative programme is license for themselves, or else restrictions for man.

(c) Next there file past the incomplete. One side of their nature has undergone atrophy, with the result that they have lost touch with their living fellow men and women.

Their programme is to convert the whole world into an epicene institution---an epicene institution in which man and woman shall everywhere work side by side at the selfsame tasks and for the selfsame pay.

These wishes can never by any possibility be realised. Even in animals--I say even, because in these at least one of the sexes has periods of complete quiscence--male and female cannot be safely worked side by side, except when they are incomplete.

While in the human species safety can be obtained, it can be obtained only at the price of continual constraint.

And even then woman, though she protests that she does not require it, and that she does not receive it, practically always does receive differential treatment at the hands of man.

It would be well, I often think, that every woman should be clearly told--and the woman of the world will immediately understand--that when man sets his face against the proposal to bring in an epicene world, he does so because he can do his best work only in surroundings where he is perfectly free from suggestion and from restraint, and from the onus which all differential treatment imposes.

And I may add in connexion with my own profession that when a medical man asks that he should not be the yoke-fellow of a medical woman he does so also because he would wish to keep up as between men and women--even when they are doctors--some of the modesties and reticences upon which our civilisation has been built up.

Now the medical woman is of course never on the side of modesty,[1] or in favour of any reticences. Her desire for knowledge does not allow of these.

[1] To those who have out of inadvertence and as laymen and women misunderstood, it may be explained that the issue here discussed is the second in order of the three which are set out on p. 139 (supra).

(d) Inextricably mixed up with the types which we have been discussing is the type of woman whom Dr. Leonard Williams's recent letter brought so distinctly before our eyes--the woman who is poisoned by her misplaced self-esteem; and who flies out at every man who does not pay homage to her intellect.

She is the woman who is affronted when a man avers that for him the glory of woman lies in her power of attraction, in her capacity for motherhood, and in unswerving allegiance to the ethics which are special to her sex.

I have heard such an intellectually embittered woman say, though she had been self-denyingly taken to wife, that "never in the whole course of her life had a man ever as much as done her a kindness."

The programme of this type of woman is, as a preliminary, to compel man to admit her claim to be his intellectual equal; and, that done, to compel him to divide up everything with her to the last farthing, and so make her also his financial equal.

And her journals exhibit to us the kind of parliamentary representative she desiderates. He humbly, hat in hand, asks for his orders from a knot of washerwomen standing arms a-kimbo.[2]

[2] I give, in response to a request, the reference: Votes for Women, March 18, 1910, p. 381.

(e) Following in the wake of these embittered human beings come troops of girls just grown up.

All these will assure you, these young girls--and what is seething in their minds is stirring also in the minds in the girls in the colleges and schools which are staffed by unmarried suffragists--that woman has suffered all manner of indignity and injustice at the hands of man.

And these young girls have been told about the intellectual, and moral, and financial value of woman--such tales as it never entered into the heart of man to conceive.

The programme of these young women is to be married upon their own terms. Man shall--so runs their scheme--work for their support--to that end giving up his freedom, and putting himself under orders, for many hours of the day; but they themselves must not be asked to give up any of their liberty to him, or to subordinate themselves to his interests, or to obey him in anything.

To obey a man would be to commit the unpardonable sin.

It is not necessary, in connexion with a movement which proceeds on the lines set out above, any further to labour the point that there is in it an element of mental disorder. It is plain that it is there.

There is also a quite fatuous element in the programmes of the militant suffragist. We have this element, for instance, in the doctrine that, notwithstanding the fact that the conditions of the labour market deny it to her, woman ought to receive the same wage as a man for the same work.

This doctrine is fatuous, because it leaves out of sight that, even if woman succeeds in doing the same work as man, he has behind him a much larger reserve of physical strength. As soon as a time of strain comes, areserve of strength and freedom from periodic indisposition is worth paying extra for.

Fatuous also is the dogma that woman ought to have the same pay for the same work--fatuous because it leaves out of sight that woman's commercial value in many of the best fields of work is subject to a very heavy discount by reason of the fact that she cannot, like a male employee, work cheek by jowl with a male employer; nor work among men as a man with his fellow employees.

So much for the woman suffragist's protest that she can conceive of no reason for a differential rate of pay for man.

Quite as fatuous are the marriage projects of the militant suffragist. Every woman of the world could tell her--whispering it into her private ear--that if a sufficient number of men should come to the conclusion that it was not worth their while to marry except on the terms of fair give-and-take, the suffragist woman's demands would have to come down.

It is not at all certain that the institution of matrimony--which, after all, is the great instrument in the levelling up of the financial situation of woman-- can endure apart from some willing subordination on the part of the wife.

It will have been observed that there is in these programmes, in addition to the element of mental disorder and to the element of the fatuous, which have been animadverted upon, also a very ugly element of dishonesty. In reality the very kernel of the militant suffrage movement is the element of immorality.

There is here not only immorality in the ends which are in view, but also in the methods adopted for the attainment of those ends.

We may restrict ourselves to indicating wherein lies the immorality of the methods.

There is no one who does not discern that woman in her relations to physical force stands in quite a different position to man.

Out of that different relation there must of necessity shape itself a special code of ethics for woman. And to violate that code must be for woman immorality.

So far as I have seen, no one in this controversy has laid his finger upon the essential point in the relations of woman to physical violence.

It has been stated--and in the main quite truly stated--that woman in the mass cannot, like man, back up her vote by bringing physical force into play.

But the woman suffragist here counters by insisting that she as an individual may have more physical force than an individual man.

And it is quite certain--and it did not need suffragist raids and window-breaking riots to demonstrate it--that woman in the mass can bring a certain amount of physical force to bear.

The true inwardness of the relation in which woman stands to physical force lies not in the question of her having it at command, but in the fact that she cannot put it forth without placing herself within the jurisdiction of an ethical law.

The law against which she offends when she resorts to physical violence is not an ordinance of man; it is not written in the statutes of any State; it has not been enunciated by any human law-giver. It belongs to those unwritten, and unassailable, and irreversible commandments of religion, [Greek 1], which we suddenly and mysteriously become aware of when we see them violated.

[1 From Antigone by Sophocles; "_the unwritten and unassailable statutes given to us by the gods._" Sir Almroth had it in the original Greek with Greek fonts.]

The law which the militant suffragist has violated is among the ordinances of that code which forbade us even to think of employing our native Indian troops against the Boers; which brands it as an ignominy when a man leaves his fellow in the lurch and saves his own life; and which makes it an outrage for a man to do violence to a woman.

To violate any ordinance of that code is more dishonourable than to transgress every statutory law.

We see acknowledgment of it in the fact that even the uneducated man in the street resents it as an outrage to civilisation when he sees a man strike a blow at a woman.

But to the man who is committing the outrage it is a thing simply unaccountable that any one should fly out at him.

In just such a case is the militant suffragist. She cannot understand why any one should think civilisation is outraged when she scuffles in the street mud with a policeman.

If she asks for an explanation, it perhaps behoves a man to supply it.

Up to the present in the whole civilised world there has ruled a truce of God as between man and woman. That truce is based upon the solemn covenant that within the frontiers of civilisation (outside them of course the rule lapses) the weapon of physical force may not be applied by man against woman; nor by woman against man.

Under this covenant, the reign of force which prevails in the world without comes to an end when a man enters his household.

Under this covenant that half of the human race which most needs protection is raised up above the waves of violence.

Within the terms of this compact everything that woman has received from man, and everything man receives from woman, is given as a free gift.

Again, under this covenant a full half of the programme of Christianity has been realised; and a foundation has been laid upon which it may be possible to build higher; and perhaps finally in the ideal future to achieve the abolition of physical violence and war.

And it is this solemn covenant, the covenant so faithfully kept by man, which has been violated by the militant suffragist in the interest of her morbid, stupid, ugly, and dishonest programmes.

Is it wonder if men feel that they have had enough of the militant suffragist, and that the State would be well rid of her if she were crushed under the soldiers' shields like the traitor woman at the Tarpeian rock [in ancient Rome where traitors were killed]?

We may turn now to that section of woman suffragists--one is almost inclined to doubt whether it any longer exists--which is opposed to all violent measures, though it numbers in its ranks women who are stung to the quick by the thought that man, who will concede the vote to the lowest and most degraded of his own sex, withholds it from "even the noblest woman in England."

When that excited and somewhat pathetic appeal is addressed to us, we have only to consider what a vote really gives.

The parliamentary vote is an instrument--and a quite astonishly disappointing instrument it is--for obtaining legislation; that is, for directing that the agents of the State shall in certain defined circumstances bring into application the weapon of physical compulsion.

Further, the vote is an instrument by which we give to this or that group of statesmen anthority to supervise and keep in motion the whole machinery of compulsion.

To take examples. A vote cast in favour of a Bill for the prohibition of alcohol--if we could find opportunity for giving a vote on such a question-- would be a formal expression of our desire to apply, through the agency of the paid servants of the State, that same physical compulsion which Mrs. Carrie Nation put into application in her "bar-smashing" crusades.

And a vote which puts a Government into office in a country where murder is punishable by death is a vote which, by agency of the hangman, puts the noose round the neck of every convicted murderer.

So that the difference between voting and direct resort to force is simply the difference between exerting physical violence in person, and exerting it through the intermediary of an agent of the State.

The thing, therefore, that is withheld from "the noblest woman in England," while it is conceded to the man who is lacking in nobility of character, is in the end only an instrument by which she might bring into application physical force.

When one realises that that same noblest woman of England would shrink from any personal exercise of violence, one would have thought that it would have come home to her that it is not precisely her job to commission a man forcibly to shut up a public-house, or to hang a murderer.

One cannot help asking oneself whether, if she understood what a vote really means, the noblest woman in England would still go on complaining of the bitter insult which is done to her in withholding the vote.

But the opportunist--the practical politician, as he calls himself--will perhaps here intervene, holding some such language as this:--"Granting all you say, granting, for the sake of argument, that the principle of giving votes to woman is unsound, and that evil must ultimately come of it, how can you get over the fact that no very conspicuous harm has resulted from woman suffrage in the countries which have adopted it? And can any firm reasons be rendered for the belief that the giving of votes to women in England would be any whit more harmful than in the Colonies?"

A very few words will supply the answer.

The evils of woman suffrage lie, first, in the fact that to give the vote to women is to give it to voters who as a class are quite incompetent to adjudicate upon political issues; secondly, in the fact that women are a class of voters who cannot effectively back up their votes by force; and, thirdly, in the fact that it may seriously embroil man and woman.

The first two aspects of the question have already in this controversy been adequately dealt with. There remains the last issue.

>From the point of view of this issue the conditions which we have to deal with in this country are the absolute antithesis of those ruling in any of the countries and States which have adopted woman suffrage.

When woman suffrage was adopted in these countries it was adopted in some for one reason, in others for another. In some it was adopted because it appealed to the doctrinaire [theoretical] politician as the proper logical outcome of a democratic and Socialistic policy. In others it was adopted because opportunist politicians saw in it an instrument by which they might gain electioneering advantages. So much was this the case that it sometimes happened that the woman's vote was sprung upon a community which was quite unprepared and indifferent to it.

The cause of woman suffrage was thus in the countries of which we speak neither in its inception nor in its realisation a question of revolt of woman against the oppression of man. It had, and has, no relation to the programmes of the militant suffragists as set out at the outset of this letter.

By virtue of this, all the evils which spring from the embroiling of man and woman have in the countries in question been conspicuously absent.

Instead of seeing himself confronted by a section of embittered and hostile women voters which might at any time outvote him and help to turn an election, man there sees his women folk voting practically everywhere in accordance with his directions, and lending him a hand to outvote his political opponent.

Whether or no such voting is for the good of the common weal is beside our present question. But it is clearly an arrangement which leads to amity and peace between a man and his womenkind, and through these to good-will towards all women.

In England everything is different.

If woman suffrage comes in here, it will have come as a surrender to a very violent feminist agitation--an agitation which we have traced back to our excess female population and the associated abnormal physiological conditions.

If ever Parliament concedes the vote to woman in England, it will be accepted by the militant suffragist, not as an eirenicon, but as a victory which she will value only for the better carrying on of her fight a outrance [to the bitter end] against the oppression and injustice of man.

A conciliation with hysterical revolt is neither an act of peace; nor will it bring peace.

Nor would the conferring of the vote upon women carry with it any advantages from the point of view of finding a way out of the material entanglements in which woman is enmeshed, and thus ending the war between man and woman.

One has only to ask oneself whether or not it would help the legislator in remodelling the divorce or the bastardy laws if he had conjoined with him an unmarried militant suffragist as assessor.

Peace will come again. It will come when woman ceases to believe and to teach all manner of evil of man despitefully. It will come when she ceases to impute to him as a crime her own natural disabilities, when she ceases to resent the fact that man cannot and does not wish to work side by side with her. And peace will return when every woman for whom there is no room in England seeks "rest" beyond the sea, "each one in the house of her husband," and when the woman who remains in England comes to recognise that she can, without sacrifice of dignity, give a willing subordination to the husband or father, who, when all is said and done, earns and lays up money for her.

A. E. WRIGHT. March 27, 1912.

www.ingramcontent.com/pod-product-compliance
Lightning Source LLC
Chambersburg PA
CBHW070401290526
45790CB00004B/1584